Backroads of Colorado
Boyd and Barbara Norton

Voyageur Press

A Pictorial Discovery Guide

Acknowledgments

There were numerous people who helped us greatly in compiling this new, revised edition of *Backroads of Colorado*. Foremost among them are our friends Sid and Marge Whitford. Long-time Colorado residents, they've traveled many a backroad here and offered to us very valuable information.

We'd also like to thank Bonnie Rose, our administrative assistant, who helped keep track of the enormous amount of information compiled. Her patient attendance to this information helped to keep it as accurate and as up to date as possible.

Sharon Kyhl, recreation forester for Pike and San Isabel National Forests, and Kathy Voth of the Grand Junction Bureau of Land Management office provided great help. And thanks to Linda Allen of the Colorado State Patrol. We're also grateful to Steve Millis of Canon City and Theresa Janssen of Glade Park for their help.

Finally, a big thanks to all of our fans of the first edition of *Backroads of Colorado* who took the time to call or write with helpful information.

Text copyright © 1995 by Boyd & Barbara Norton
Road map of Colorado on page 8 from the *Deluxe Road Atlas & Travel Guide*
copyright © 1995 by Rand McNally, R.L. 95-S-113

All rights reserved. No part of this work may be reproduced or used in any form by any means—graphic, electronic, or mechanical, including photocopying, recording, taping, or any information storage and retrieval system—without written permission of the publisher.

Edited by Michael Dregni • Designed by Kathryn Mallien and Andrea Rud
Printed in Hong Kong
98 99 00 01 02 6 5 4 3

Library of Congress Cataloging-in-Publication Data
Norton, Boyd.
    Backroads of Colorado / by Boyd and Barbara Norton. — New rev. ed.
        p.   cm.
    Includes bibliographical references and index.
    ISBN 0-89658-316-3
        1. Colorado—Guidebooks. 2. Automobile travel—Colorado—Guidebooks.
    3. Colorado—History—Miscellanea. I. Norton, Barbara. II. Title.
    F774.3.N67   1995
    917.8804'33—dc20   95-7222
                                                             CIP

Distributed in Canada by Raincoast Books, 8680 Cambie Street, Vancouver, B.C. V6P 6M9

Published by Voyageur Press, Inc.
P.O. Box 338, 123 North Second Street, Stillwater, MN 55082 U.S.A.
651-430-2210, fax 651-430-2211

Please write or call, or stop by, for our free catalog of natural history publications.
Our toll-free number to place an order or to obtain a free catalog is 800-888-WOLF (800-888-9653).
Educators, fundraisers, premium and gift buyers, publicists, and marketing managers: Looking for creative products and new sales ideas? Voyageur Press books are available at special discounts when purchased in quantities, and special editions can be created to your specifications. For details contact our marketing department.

Page 1: *Backroad wandering through an aspen forest in the Telluride region*

Contents

Introduction to the Original Edition

▲▲▲▲▲

Today's modern interstate highways are a boon to the American traveler, making it fast and easy to get from Point A to Point B. Let's face it, we all use them, and I'm no different, being as impatient as anyone else to reach my destination.

The trouble with interstates is that in addition to being convenient they are also boring, frustrating, and deceptive. The tedium of mile after speeding mile is broken only by rest stops and exits for gas, food, or lodging. But even these respites do little to alleviate the overall boredom. The frustration comes when you spot local features and landmarks that you'd like a closer look at, only to discover there is no handy escape from this linear imprisonment. By the time you do find an exit, your initial enthusiasm has usually waned. And, finally, it's easy to be fooled in your impressions of a given land when you view it over guardrails swishing by at fifty-five per. The real flavor of a place can only be gained by wandering leisurely, talking to people, smelling, feeling, tasting the land at close range and slow pace.

In short, interstates may give us velocity, but only backroads can give us roots.

Doorway of old building in the ghost town of Como in the South Park region

Ever since I moved to the Rockies more than three decades ago, I've been a sucker for backroads. The obscure, unmarked lane—sometimes it's only two wheel ruts winding off over the hill or out of sight through the forest—is too much of a temptation for me to pass up. I *have* to find out where it goes and why. So with squealing brakes, a tight turn, and a cloud of dust, I'm off. Sometimes, after hours of teeth-rattling, bone-jarring travel, the road simply ends in the middle of nowhere, with no evidence as to why it existed to begin with. Other times the reward at the end of the long, slow journey is some special place. A secret lake. A magnificent view. An enchanted forest. Some exciting bit of history or prehistory. Even though I'm an ardent backpacker and wilderness fanatic, I must confess that some of my greatest personal discoveries were made from a vehicle, bouncing madly over a dirt road in the middle of terra incognita.

Right off I should point out that there are backroads and there are godawful backroads in Colorado. The former are merely fun, the latter adventur-

Aspen forest along Old Lime Creek Road in the Silverton-Ouray region ous and often hair-raising. Many of them follow the original pathways of a century or more ago, their condition improved only a little since then—and sometimes not at all. I would be rich if I had been paid by the hour for all the time I've spent lost, stuck, or groaning interminably in low gear over some miserable rutted track.

I should mention I never use a Jeep-type four-wheel-drive vehicle. When the going gets that rough, I usually prefer to walk. Besides, feet are easier on the land where there are no roads. So the backroads here are those we've driven ourselves, Barbara and I, in normal vehicles ranging from a plain old garden-variety Dodge van to a Toyota Tercel and a Honda Civic. Though the Toyota is a four-wheel-drive station wagon, I've rarely used the four-wheel drive, except in winter. A great many of the backroads described here don't require four-wheel drive. Many, however, do require some decent ground clearance, an essential feature for any vehicle to be used for extensive backroad driving in Colorado.

Not all the backroads are rough, unpaved tracks, and some of them may surprise you. For example, U.S. Highway 6 used to be the main, heavily traveled route over the Continental Divide at Loveland Pass. With the completion of Interstate 70 and the Eisenhower Memorial Tunnel, the spectacular and beautiful Loveland Pass route has been relegated to the rank of a backroad, used by relatively few people. There are those of us, however, who prefer it to the modern highway.

But whether the route you plan to follow into the back country takes you over a paved highway or a pair of wheel ruts, before taking off it is always advisable to make local inquiry as to the condition of the roads—especially in mountainous areas. It can save a lot of grief and backtracking. It's also a good idea to take along a shovel, a tool kit, a set of tire chains, and perhaps an extra fan belt. A jug or two of water and several extra cans of beans may also be reassuring items in case you find yourself stuck and benighted by a late or early seasonal storm, as I have on occasion. And be sure the spare tire has air in it.

Backroads of Colorado is not intended to be a guidebook. What I hope to convey here is more in the way of inspiration—blended with some useful information in the form of essays, photos, and maps—to seek real adventure, to explore and savor the Colorado back country as I have. The mini-tours described here by no means cover the entire state. It would take more than one lifetime to explore all the out-of-the-way places and backroads of Colorado. Besides, there are a few spots I'm keeping secret. You may find these yourself, and if you do, they'll be that much more special.

These mini-tours include a sampling of all that the Colorado landscape has to offer: mountain, in the High Country; desert, in the Colorado Plateau area; and prairie, in the Great Plains. Each is fascinating in its history and beauty. So I urge you to resist the temptation to spend all your time in the rugged mountain country, and explore the state's other domains.

For the purposes of this book, I've arbitrarily divided the state into three regions: the High Country, the Western Slopes, and the Great Plains. Coloradans call the entire section on the western side of the Continental Divide—including portions of the High Country and all of the Colorado Plateau—the Western Slopes, but here I've used the term to mean roughly the western third of Colorado from a line drawn north to south through Glenwood Springs. In general, the length of the traveling season is the determining factor for this arrangement.

Each region is covered separately, beginning with an introduction in which the physical features are described and the driving seasons explained. Bad weather can ruin your trip; at the least it can take the fun out of it. You can't always foresee weather hazards, of course, but the general guidelines I've mentioned should be helpful.

Every mini-tour is mapped, and for orientation, there is also a full-page map of the state showing all the cities and the principal roads. If you would like to find other backroads on your own, you can start by writing for the U.S. Geological Survey maps available from the Interior Geological Survey Office, Denver Federal Center, West 6th Avenue and Kipling, Denver, CO 80225. Ask for a master index. Or, better yet, if you are passing through the Denver area, it's worth a side trip to visit the office and browse through the great collection of maps. From a personal standpoint, I find the National Topographic Maps—1:250,000 series—to be the most practical and useful.

As a final note, this book entitles you to a free membership in the SPB, the Society for the Preservation of Backroads. I suppose there's not much danger of changing some of the roads described here, but I'm always saddened when I return to a place and find that the heavy hand of progress has altered it detrimentally

Sangre de Cristo Range and the Wet Mountain Valley

and often at an unnecessary expenditure of time, money, and energy. I like the idea that for the really adventurous there will always be out-of-the-way places difficult to access. Joseph Wood Krutch summed up the lure of the backroad perfectly: "Rough roads act as filters," he once wrote. "The rougher the road, the finer the filter."

Those who care will make it.

Boyd Norton
Evergreen, Colorado

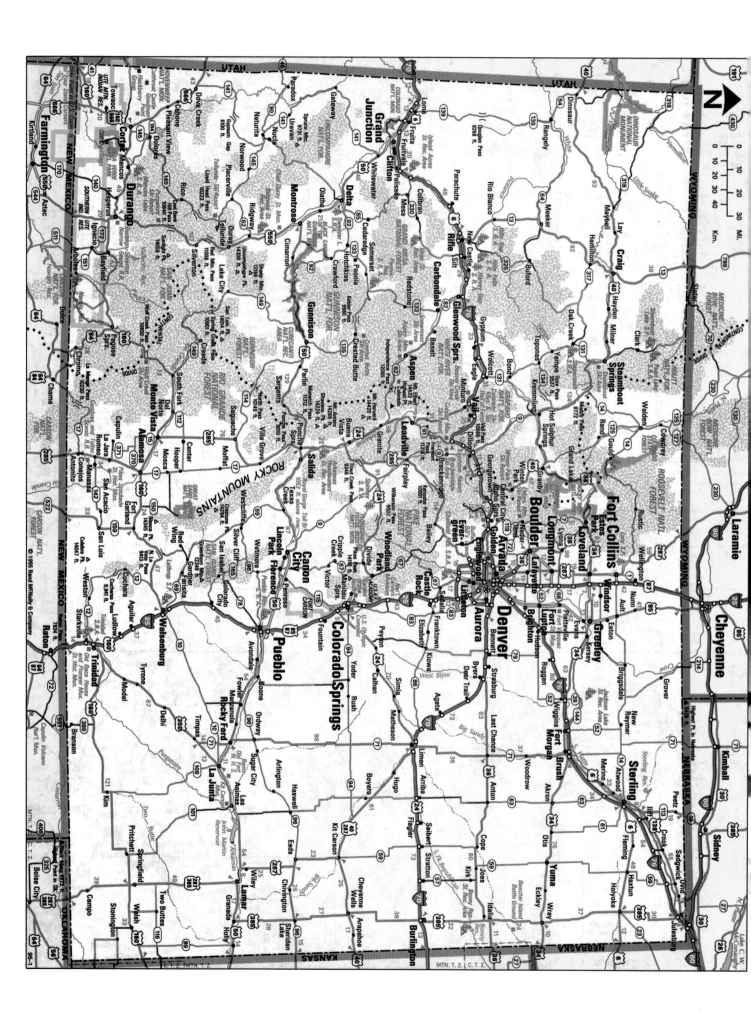

Introduction to the New Revised Edition

▲▲▲▲▲

When *Backroads of Colorado* was first published by Rand McNally in spring 1978, we had no idea that it would be so popular. In fact, we were somewhat surprised, if not shocked, to see it on the *Denver Post*'s best-seller list for twenty-three consecutive weeks. Eight printings and nearly ninety thousand copies later, the reality set in: There are a lot of people who share with us the idea that the slowest way of getting from Point A to Point B is often the best way.

We were also gratified that so many people took time to write or phone, expressing their enjoyment of the book. Many of these people enthusiastically shared with us their own personal adventures. And some of the suggestions have been incorporated into this new edition.

In the intervening years, we've experienced other backroads in various parts of the world, and we can personally attest to the fact that Colorado's are, for the most part, reasonably well maintained. That's true when compared to say, Siberia or parts of Africa. We still hold painful memories of being bogged down in mud up to the doors, on what passes for a road in Sikhote Alinsky in eastern Siberia. And the time we were

Early summer needle buds on a blue spruce tree in the San Juan Mountains

caught in the beginning of the rainy season in southern Kenya, when the road turned to unimaginable goo and required pushing and pulling the vehicle every hundred yards. (We returned to Nairobi so coated in mud that it threatened to clog the hotel's shower drains.)

That's not to say that such things can't happen in Colorado. There are still some backroads that require caution, especially at certain times of the year and in certain weather conditions. As we advised in the first edition, always make local inquiries if you aren't sure about a particular road. And carry emergency supplies such as flares, extra water and gas, food, and blankets. Adventure is still there for the adventurous, although it's always wise to make it as nonlethal as possible.

Things change. Since the first edition of *Backroads of Colorado* there have been some alterations in the places described. Fortunately, not too many drastic changes have occurred. Many, if not most, of the backroad tours are still that—quiet, out-of-the-way trips where you can still experience the beauty and peacefulness of Colorado. The descriptions here reflect any changes that we've noted ourselves or that others have reported to us.

Above: *Eagle River Valley from the road to Heart Lake in the White River National Forest*
Opposite: *Abandoned ore-loading chute near Central City*

One positive change that we've noted over the years is the closure of certain areas, particularly in the delicate alpine country, to off-road vehicles. There have been far too many abuses, and the damage already caused will be decades, if not centuries, in healing. In most places, off-roading is not only intolerable, but unnecessary. There are plenty of existing backroads to satisfy any wanderlust without the necessity of creating a multitude of new tracks. The whole idea of following backroads is to get to a place where you can enjoy the beauty of Colorado. But that's hard to do if the land is scarred by thoughtless people.

Judging from the people who responded to the first edition of *Backroads of Colorado*, there are a lot who share this same philosophy. And so we dedicate this book to all of you who revel in the mystery and challenge of following that obscure road out to the back of beyond, just to see what's there and to get out of the vehicle at road's end and enjoy the sweet land.

Happy backroading!

Boyd and Barbara Norton
Evergreen, Colorado

Part I
The High Country
▲▲▲▲▲

The High Country is the region for which Colorado is most famous. Rock-ribbed barriers thrust high into the deep blue sky. Snow. Tundra. Glaciated cirques and basins. Swift, brawling mountain streams. Forests of pine, spruce, and aspen. Clear, crisp air. Country still clean, pure, and wild.

Colorado is the highest of the fifty states, with fifty-five peaks soaring more than 14,000 feet above sea level. Alaska has taller mountains—Mount McKinley is almost 6,000 feet higher than Mount Elbert, Colorado's highest peak—but Colorado's average elevation is 6,800 feet, while Alaska's is only 1,900. The lowest point in Colorado is 3,350 feet above sea level, whereas parts of Alaska are at sea level. Colorado boasts a city, Leadville, that is almost 2 miles high. And Colorado's mountains, although dwarfed by Mount McKinley, are giants in comparison to those east of the Mississippi, where the highest point, Mount Mitchell in the Appalachians, rises only 6,684 feet above sea level.

About half of Colorado lies within the Rockies. As you approach them from the eastern plains, the mountains seem to form a continuous, impenetrable

Crystal River near Aspen in autumn

barrier. You soon learn, however, that there are numerous routes and passes allowing relatively easy traverse from east to west. You also discover that the Colorado Rockies are not a single chain of mountains at all, but a series of distinct ranges, sometimes interconnected, sometimes separated by wide valleys, plateaus, and vast high swales, or basins, appropriately called "parks" by early explorers. These grassy natural parks include the San Luis Valley, North Park, Middle Park, and South Park.

The backbone of Colorado's High Country forms part of the Continental Divide, which separates streams draining to the east from those draining to the west. The divide runs through the state from north to south. Here accumulated waters flowing to the east reach the Gulf of Mexico by way of the Arkansas, the South Platte, and the Rio Grande. Drainage to the Pacific Ocean is through the Colorado River system.

Geologically the Rockies are considered young mountains. Although not all the ranges comprising the Rocky Mountain chain are the same age, most of those in Colorado are sixty million to seventy million years old. There was no single, cataclysmic upthrust

Indian paintbrush summer blossoms in the San Juan Mountains

*Crossing Mosquito Pass at the head of Evans Gulch, northwest of Fairplay, with a horsedrawn wagon, circa 1900
(Photo courtesy of Library, The State Historical Society of Colorado)*

that formed these ranges. Instead, slow, intermittent movements of the earth's crust produced the folding and buckling that raised the bedrock gradually higher over millennia of time. And while the restless earth raised ever so slowly, counterforces in the form of ice and water eroded and corroded these mountains, transporting the scourings grain by grain to the distant plains and even more distant oceans. Glaciers during the last three ice ages sculpted and faceted many of the peaks into the sharp jagged shapes so noticeable in many places today.

The High Country is also the gold and silver country that lured hordes of fortune seekers to Colorado in the last century. Many of the backroads that wind through canyons and twist in tortuous switchbacks up ridges and over passes follow the paths made by the prospectors. A few of the roads are old railroad beds of now-defunct lines that once brought passengers to long-gone mining towns and carried out ore. Obviously, this can be tough, axle-breaking country to drive in, but the grandeur of the scenery is worth it. You can also absorb some of the region's history in visiting the tumbledown buildings of old boomtowns now being reclaimed by the elements.

For all its outward ruggedness, this is delicate country. Many of the roads will lead you far above tree line and into the strange and beautiful world of alpine tundra. In July and August the display of wildflowers is nothing short of spectacular. But increased motorized mobility in recent decades has begun to leave its mark. Wheel ruts become scars that may last for centuries on the slow-healing tundra. Because of the harsh climate and short growing season, some species of alpine plants may take as long as two decades to germinate, grow, flower, and reproduce. So keep your vehicle on established roads and, when hiking, stick to regular trails. Even in forested lower elevations, serious damage can occur when vehicles are used thoughtlessly.

The season for traveling the backroads of the High Country is relatively short. Many, if not most, of them are open only during the summer months. And here, summer means July and August, and occasionally part

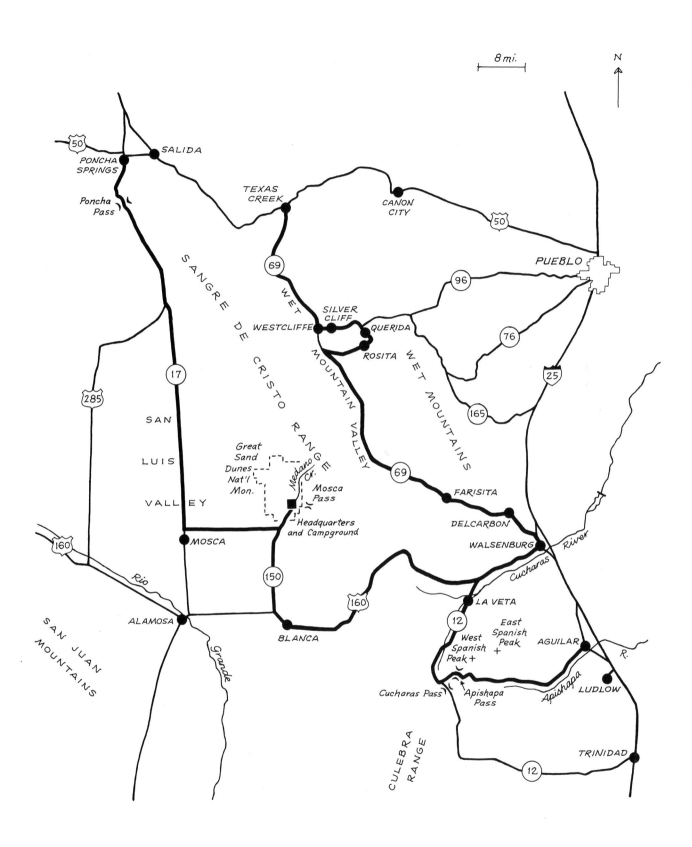

The Spanish Peaks, Ludlow, Great Sand Dunes National Monument, and the Wet Mountain Valley

North Fork of Lake Creek from Independence Pass

of September. There are year-to-year variations, however, so always inquire locally before heading off into unfamiliar territory. A particular road that is accessible most years by the first of July may, in winters of heavy snow, be impassable until mid-July.

Sudden changes in the weather can also be a problem in the High Country. Even on days that begin clear and cloudless, storms may move in by early or mid-afternoon. Rocky Mountain storms can be severe, often violent as evidenced by the tragic flash flood in Big Thompson Canyon that killed more than 130 people in 1976. Fortunately, such disasters are rare, but it is wise not to underestimate the potential dangers of mountain storms. When traveling in the High Country, keep an eye on gathering cloud formations. The small, puffy white cumulus clouds represent no threat, but take heed when they begin to coalesce into big, convoluted and dark cumulonimbus, or thunderclouds. Unless your view is blocked by nearby peaks or ridges, you often have warning of an impending storm. Such storms usually move in from the west or southwest in most of Colorado's High Country.

What do you do when the weather turns bad? In general, avoid the high, open expanses above timberline. If you should be caught at high elevations during a severe storm, stay put. Driving rain, sleet, or hail can make negotiating those tortuous roads extremely hazardous. Most of these storms are brief, and chances are that in an hour or so the sun will be shining again. Your car offers the best protection against lightning. But if you can't get back to your vehicle, there are a few important precautions that will minimize danger from lightning: Stay off exposed ridges and high peaks. Separate yourself from any metal-framed packs by a reasonable distance. Don't seek shelter under a tree. Lie flat on the ground and stay there until the storm passes.

For purposes of planning your own backroad trips in this area, it is worth a stop at Maps Unlimited, 9th and Broadway in Denver. They have excellent maps of all kinds, including U.S. Forest Service and U.S. Geological Survey maps.

The Spanish Peaks

I like this trip because it has a variety of things to offer: flat, arid country, stately old forests, interesting geology, mountain streams and wildflowers, alpine spectacles, scenic vistas, pleasant ranch country, and the legend of lost Spanish gold. It also has a rather abrupt elevation change—almost a vertical mile—in a relatively short distance, bringing you up to 11,000 feet and near timberline.

Take U.S. Highway 160 at Walsenburg, drive west about fourteen miles, then turn south onto Colorado Highway 12, which runs along the Cucharas River. (*Cuchara* in Spanish means "spoon," the name apparently applied here because of the concave shape of the valley where the stream originates.) To the south are West and East Spanish Peaks (13,623 and 12,669 feet in elevation respectively), twin mountains that stand away from the Culebra Range to the west. The Indians called them *Huajatolla*, or "Breasts of the World." The Utes believed them to be the home of fearsome gods and avoided them.

The legend of lost Spanish gold goes back to 1541, when Spanish conquistador Francisco Vásquez de Coronado journeyed through southwestern Colorado. On his return to Mexico, he left three of his priests in northern New Mexico to spread Christianity among the Indians. One of those priests, Fray Juan de la Cruz, traveled north to Huajatolla where he heard reports of rich Indian mines there. According to legend, the priest found fabulous treasures, loaded his mules with as much gold as they could carry, and set out for New Mexico. He was never seen or heard from again. In the mid-1800s, stories of lost Spanish gold continued to trickle out of these mountains and were repeated in such places as Bent's Fort in the plains east of here, but thus far the rich mines—if they ever existed—remain hidden in the Spanish Peaks country.

This area has a decided Spanish flavor to it, as you'll note in passing through the town of La Veta, which lies at the foot of the two mountains. *La Veta* is Spanish for "the vein"; in the early years of settlement, a vein of white mineral was crushed and used as whitewash for the adobe houses and buildings.

Soon the highway enters the southern extension of the San Isabel National Forest and you have a view of an unusual geological feature. On the flanks of the Spanish Peaks are tall fins, or walls, that run for miles up and down the foothills and bear a resemblance to the Great Wall of China. These entities are dikes, intrusive veins of hard igneous rock that have remained behind while softer surrounding rock has worn away.

Before long the road begins rising steeply and curving in ever-tighter switchbacks. At Cucharas Pass (elevation 9,994 feet) there's a gravel road to the left that leads to the higher Apishapa Pass (elevation 11,005 feet). As you climb this road, there are stunning views to the west and southwest of the Culebra Range, perhaps the only large mountain range in Colorado that is not part of the national forests. (*Culebra*, incidentally, is Spanish for "snake.") Near Apishapa Pass, West Spanish Peak looms several thousand feet above you.

At the top of the pass I spent several hours roaming around amid stunted alpine fir and meadow flowers. Apishapa Pass isn't quite at timberline, but it's close. Few people realize that the elevation at which trees cease to grow depends on both climate and exposure. Sometimes it can vary a thousand feet or more on a single mountain, with the milder south-facing slope retaining trees higher than the harsher north

slope. In Colorado, the average elevation of the timberline is about 11,000 feet, but in these southern mountains, where the climate is milder, it can be 12,000 feet or even higher. In some places in the colder northern Rockies, timberline is often as low as 9,000 feet.

An approaching thunderstorm forced me to move on. Rather than retracing my path, I continued down the east side of Apishapa Pass and was treated to magnificent views of rolling hills and prairie country far off to the southeast toward Raton Pass and New Mexico. Somewhere out there, I thought to myself, may be buried the treasure of Fray de la Cruz. But it would take several lifetimes to search those thousands of square miles.

Once more in the lowlands, the road winds through typical arid country where you'll again notice a strong Spanish influence in the architecture. One strange thing about the area near Aguilar: Someone spent an awful lot of time and energy in nailing old license plates to road posts. There are miles and miles of them. About six miles south of Aguilar is the site of the infamous "Ludlow Massacre."

Great Sand Dunes National Monument

In my travels throughout the West, I've found several mountain valleys that have a special charm and beauty: Jackson Hole in Wyoming, the Bitterroot Valley of Montana, Teton Valley and Stanley Basin in Idaho. Ranked high among these is the San Luis Valley, which also happens to be the largest of the natural parks in the Colorado Rockies. Flanked by the rugged Sangre de Cristo Range on the east and by the San Juan and La Garita Mountains on the west, this broad valley averages about 7,500 feet above sea level and is dotted with numerous ranches and farms. But to me its chief attraction and fascination is Great Sand Dunes National Monument, a ten-mile-long stretch of shifting, varicolored sands.

Sand dunes are obviously created by wind and aridity, and one thinks of them as characteristic of desert country like the Sahara or Death Valley. "But where did all the sand come from?" is probably the

Left: *Cucharas River Valley and the Spanish Peaks*
Overleaf: *Sand dunes in the Great Sand Dunes National Monument, with the Sangre de Cristo Range in the far distance*

Ludlow

Ludlow doesn't exist. It never did exist—as a town, that is. It was just one more watering stop on the Colorado and Southern Railroad, which transported coal from the Trinidad coal fields that lay between and to the west of Walsenburg and Trinidad. Almost no one outside of Colorado had ever heard of it until April 20, 1914. Then it became famous—or infamous—in a hurry.

Life for a Colorado coal miner in 1913 was not pleasant. Even if he managed to work the average of two hundred days and thus earn seven hundred dollars per year, the company was always there to take it back. There was the company house rental, the company store, the company health insurance. And the company levied charges for blacksmithing and explosives.

The miner had no rights. The company ruled every aspect of his life, from what teacher his children had to what books he was allowed to read.

He worked under appalling safety conditions, yet each and every accident was ruled to be the fault of the miner: "If he were more careful, he wouldn't have been hurt." And he could expect no help from the local or state government. They were as tightly controlled by the Colorado Fuel and Iron Company as was the miner.

His only salvation was the union. And so, in spite of the beatings administered to union organizers by the thugs that were hired by the company, the secret United Mine Workers' membership list grew.

By September 1913, the coal miners had had enough. The union called for a strike and some eight thousand miners walked out. They moved their families out of the company towns on the mountain slopes to tent colonies on the plains and settled in for what was to become a bitter and bloody struggle.

Ludlow was the largest of the tent colonies. Several incidents there served as an excuse to call out the Colorado National Guard, under the command of the vigorously anti-union General John Chase. By April, the guard had made four raids on Ludlow.

No one really knows who started the battle that day after Easter, the miners or the guardsmen. For Patricia Valdez and her four children, Cedelina Costa and her two children, the two Pedregon children, and the three Petrucci children, it didn't make much difference. They took refuge from the flying bullets in an underground pit, and eleven of them suffocated when the National Guardsmen burned the tent colony to the ground over their heads.

There were other deaths that day, at least twenty in all, but the world was especially horrified by the deaths of the women and children. The press referred to the tragic incident as the "Ludlow Massacre."

The strike ended in December 1914. The miners, for all practical purposes, lost. In 1917, the United Mine Workers erected an imposing monument on the site of the death pit, but as the years went by everyone seemed to forget the massacre.

Everyone that is except Mary Petrucci and Alcarita Pedregon, the only survivors of the death pit. And they would never forget.

The death pit at the miners' Ludlow Tent Colony, following the fire of 1914 (Photo courtesy Library, The State Historical Society of Colorado)

most frequent question asked of rangers at Great Sand Dunes National Monument. It's not as foolish a question as you might suppose, for though the valley does seem somewhat dry, the many green farms and ranches belie its true arid nature. (Most of the farms are irrigated with water from deep wells.) It simply doesn't look like desert and sand dunes country. But it is. Average annual rainfall is less than ten inches here (precipitation of ten inches or less generally defines a desert). And even though its high elevation makes it a cold desert in winter, it is a desert nonetheless.

But what about the sand? Where did it come from? And why is it piled up here in dunes that are almost seven hundred feet high at the eastern edge of the valley? In large part, the San Juan and La Garita Mountains are responsible for the supply of finely ground rock that built the dunes. More than ten thousand years ago, during the last ice age, scouring ice chipped and eroded the bedrock of igneous formations in these mountains. With infinite slowness, the rivers of ice moved downwards from higher elevations, grinding and abrading as they went. Rushing streams continued the erosion process during and after the glaciation, transporting the sediment to the lowland valley. A large part of it was carried by the Rio Grande flowing through the southwest part of the San Luis Valley, and over eons of time the river gradually shifted southward, leaving dry, sandy streambeds behind.

Wind was the force that created the great dunes from this raw material. Strong southwesterly winds prevail here, and the sand has been transported across the valley to the present location of the dunes. The final factor for their creation was the great barrier of the Sangre de Cristo Range. The roaring winds, seeking the easiest flow, were funneled through gaps in the range, and as they raised up over the ramparts, their lessened velocity caused the sand to be dropped. Today, in the southeast corner of the San Luis Valley, about fifty-seven square miles of dunes have been formed and are preserved as part of the National Park System.

To reach the area, start at Walsenburg and take U.S. Highway 160 west, then just beyond the town of Blanca turn north onto Colorado Highway 150, which heads directly to the monument. If you're coming from the north, you can take U.S. Highway 285 over Poncha Pass (elevation 9,010 feet), then Colorado Highway 17 south toward Alamosa. You'll intersect a road just north of Mosca that leads you east to the dunes. By either approach the road into the national monument is a dead end. Once there, however, you can leave the campground and take some short, easy hikes into diverse and fascinating country.

My favorite hike is north along Medano Creek, which flows along the east face of the great dunes. In May and June the creek is generally running well, but later in the summer it may be dry. As soon as I reach the creek I always take off my boots and walk barefoot in the ankle-deep water. You quickly discover that the dunes are not as completely sterile and lifeless as they appear from a distance. There are various kinds of small plants and grasses; in July there is a showy display of yellow sunflowers. In a few places cottonwood trees have taken root in the sand and seem to be holding their own, somehow.

Medano Creek is an ecological interface between the arid dunes and the semi-arid foothills where grass, sage, juniper, and piñon pines grow profusely. If you slosh along here in early morning or at dusk, you're likely to see mule deer coming down to drink from the stream. A few miles north of the campground and on the east side of the creek is the Ghost Forest, an area of dead ponderosa pines. Encroaching sand dunes have killed the trees, and the sleek, silvery remains look like surrealistic sculptures.

Another favorite hike is the trail to Mosca Pass, east of the monument headquarters and campground, where you ascend through lusher montane vegetation such as aspen and spruce. A wagon trail used to cross over the pass, and you can still see traces of the old tollhouse and stage station.

Be sure to spend time at the visitor center of Great Sand Dunes National Monument to learn about these and other hikes in the area. And don't venture too far off the beaten path. The dunes can be extremely disorienting—in fact, there are legends about sheep herds and wagon trains completely disappearing here.

The Wet Mountain Valley

About halfway between Canon City and Salida on U.S. Highway 50, Colorado Highway 69 branches off to the south at the town of Texas Creek. This is a magnificent drive, for it parallels the scenic Sangre de Cristo Range to the west for many miles. (According to one story, the name *Sangre de Cristo*—Spanish for "Blood of Christ"—is derived from the utterance of a Spanish explorer when he saw a sunrise over the mountains.) This eastern side of the Sangre de Cristos,

Above: *Sangre de Cristo Range and the Wet Mountain Valley from Highway 69 near Westcliffe*
Opposite: *Mule deer doe in San Luis Valley in the Great Sand Dunes National Monument*

known as the Wet Mountain Valley, is far less traveled than the San Luis Valley on the west, though no less spectacular. To the east are the Wet Mountains. Why the name Wet? Presumably some early explorers or trappers named them: After trekking over the hot, dry plains east of Pueblo, they encountered their first storms and green slopes here in these mountains, which are now part of the eastern unit of the San Isabel National Forest.

About twenty miles south of Texas Creek, turn left at Westcliffe and follow Colorado Highway 96 east to Silver Cliff, a shadow of what was once a typical boomtown in the era of silver and gold mining. Incorporated in 1879, Silver Cliff became Colorado's third-largest city within two years, but its population plummeted in the 1890s with the drop in silver prices.

The abandoned mines are still in evidence along the hills and cliff faces. East of Silver Cliff, an unnumbered road leads south to Querida and Rosita, both now ghost towns as well. You can follow this road west to intersect Highway 69 again.

In continuing southeast on Highway 69, you somehow have the feeling of spacious, wide-open country even though there are mountain ranges on either side of you. Several roads branch off and head toward U.S. Forest Service campgrounds and small lakes tucked in the folds of the mountains.

As you leave the Sangre de Cristos farther behind and approach Walsenburg, you notice that there is an increasingly Spanish flavor to the towns and ranches. At Farisita and Delcarbon I found some marvelous old adobe buildings and a few newer ones. You also discover that you've made a transition from high mountain valley to broad, open foothills of piñon pine and juniper.

Headwaters of the Rio Grande

Not many people realize that the Rio Grande, or "Great River," which forms the border between the United States and Mexico, has its origins in the Colorado Rockies. Furthermore, the river here has a far different character than in the desert and canyon country of Texas.

About sixteen miles west of Del Norte on U.S. Highway 160, Colorado Highway 149 heads northwest from the little village of South Fork and follows the Rio Grande upstream. The river here is a typical mountain stream—broad, swift, shallow, and with excellent trout fishing. A few miles from South Fork, the valley becomes hemmed in by cliffs of angular basaltic columns. At the place where the valley is especially narrow, you'll come to the town of Wagon Wheel Gap. The town is believed to be named after an incident in the early years when a wagon was wrecked and abandoned here by prospectors fleeing attacking Indians. This area along the Rio Grande Valley has wonderful old cottonwood trees that blaze with color in the fall. It's especially nice to find a quiet place by the river and listen to the wind in the trees while basking in the warm autumn sun. This is dude ranch country, and pack trips can be arranged into the La Garita National Wilderness north of here or the Weminuche National Wilderness in the San Juan Mountains south of the valley.

Continuing on Highway 149 you come to the town of Creede, named for prospector Nicholas C. Creede, who discovered silver in 1890 and set off a stampede to the area. This is one of the most infamous boomtowns of the West's mining era. "There is no night in Creede," was a motto reflecting the rip-roaring atmosphere when miners poured into town at any time of day or night to wash away their cares in the numerous saloons. One of the noted landmarks of Creede was Ford's Saloon, built by Bob Ford, the man who shot Jesse James. Ford reputedly partook of his own wares quite frequently and on numerous occasions shot up the town in a drunken frenzy. But he died here as violently as he lived, shot in the back in his own saloon. The old building has been torn down.

The setting for the town is magnificent, with cliffs rising almost 1,000 feet above the narrow valley.

Colorado's most famous cannibal, Alferd Packer (Photo courtesy of Library, The State Historical Society of Colorado)

Creede's population reached a peak of ten thousand in the early 1890s and attracted a number of other notorious characters, among them Bat Masterson and Calamity Jane. The flashy and dapper Masterson was a faro dealer in a saloon owned by Soapy Smith; Soapy was one of the more successful con men of the day.

Like all boomtowns, Creede experienced the depletion of its ores, and soon the whole lusty population pulled up stakes and moved on, following rumors of the newest strikes. Today the town is experiencing a new boom in the form of tourism, and with it a growth in population. The numerous shops and restaurants in restored old buildings do a thriving business.

About fifteen miles west of Creede the road branches. Highway 149 heads north, and over the Continental Divide, to Lake City. The gravel road to the left leads west to the Rio Grande Reservoir, where there are several excellent U.S. Forest Service campgrounds. At the end of the road, trails lead into the Weminuche Wilderness, Colorado's largest preserved national wilderness. Here it's possible to follow the

Alferd Packer

There's a college cafeteria named after him. At least one society, its members dedicated to serving humanity, bears his name, as does a wilderness cookbook. For a time, before people began making a fuss about it, the U.S. Department of Agriculture cafeteria in Washington, D.C., was named in his honor. He was one of Colorado's most famous citizens. He was a cannibal.

Alferd Packer's story changed so many times no one can really be sure what happened that winter of 1874 near present-day Lake City. When he first staggered into the Los Pinos Indian Agency on April 16, he said he had become separated from his five companions and had been wandering around in the snow for weeks, starving. Fine. Things like that were always happening during Colorado's winters. But discrepancies in his story started to appear.

Well, he admitted under more direct questioning, that what actually happened was that they were starving to death, so when the oldest of the group died, they boiled up a bit of him to survive. The survivors ate the dead one by one. Finally, there were three left alive. One of them shot another man and then went after Alferd. Naturally, Alferd had to kill him in self defense.

Now, everyone was pretty upset about this latest confession. Killings were common in territorial Colorado. And a little self defense could be forgiven. But cannibalism, never! Why, it just wasn't done.

So Alferd Packer was arrested, but before he could be tried, he escaped and was on the lam for nine years. Then he was recognized in Wyoming and brought back to Colorado for trial.

Forget the last story, he now said. This is the true one. This is how it began: In Utah, Alferd Packer joined up with a group of twenty-one prospectors who were going to the Colorado gold fields. They damn near didn't make it. Luckily, they came upon the camp of Chief Ouray and his tribe of Utes who extended the hospitality of the camp to the prospectors for the winter. Packer and five others got itchy feet and left to push on to the gold fields. They had provisions for a week, but a snowstorm stopped them, and they ran out of food. They even ate their moccasins. Finally, Packer left camp to see if he could find something to eat. When he returned, he saw one man cooking a piece of meat over the fire. The man attacked Packer so Packer had to kill him. It was only then that he saw the bodies of the others. And guess where that piece of meat came from? Packer was so hungry he couldn't help himself—he ate the cooked meat. He stayed there for about two months until he could get through the deep snow to the Indian Agency.

The jury didn't like this story any better. He was convicted of manslaughter and sentenced to hang. Through a technicality, he was granted a retrial, but everyone knew how it would turn out. They didn't even bother to make a transcript of the proceedings.

Alferd Packer got forty years—eight years for each victim. He served seventeen years of the sentence until public sentiment forced the governor to pardon him in 1901. He died in 1907.

Right to the end he swore that he'd only killed one of his companions, not all of them. He never did deny that he'd eaten them.

In 1989, a forensic archaeology expedition composed of archaeology, anthropology, pathology, and firearms experts unearthed the bones of the victims. The bodies, they found, had definitely been cannibalized as shown by knife marks on the bones. The team leader, Dr. James Starrs, a professor of law and forensics, reported that the wounds on the bones "were caused by a hatchetlike instrument at a time when these persons were defending themselves from the attack of an aggressor." There was no doubt in Starrs's mind that the aggressor was indeed Packer. So the evidence seems to show that Packer deliberately killed his companion—all of them. There was little evidence to indicate he killed only one in self-defense as he alleged.

Of course, it's still true that he never denied eating them.

sparkling waters of the "Great River" to their origins.

Lake Fork and Lake City

West of Gunnison, U.S. Highway 50 runs into the Curecanti National Recreation Area. Just before you reach Blue Mesa Reservoir in the area, turn left on Colorado Highway 149. This first part of the trip is in dry, open sagebrush country, but gradually the land changes as you head south and southwest, climbing along low foothills. About twenty-five miles from the main highway, the transition becomes abrupt as you pass between two high, steep cliffs know as "The Gate," which pinch off the valley of the Lake Fork. Now the air becomes perfumed by spruce and pine rather than sagebrush, and you get views of the High Country spreading out to the south.

Lake Fork is a beautiful stream, clean and pure.

There are numerous places where you can pull off and walk down to the cold waters to try your hand with a fly rod or just to loaf to the music of mountain waters.

About five miles south of The Gate is the turnoff for another of those great side trips. Watch for U.S. Forest Service signs pointing the way to Big Blue Campground. This side road climbs steeply up from the valley of the Lake Fork and twists through aspen forests and stands of Douglas fir. Topping a low pass, it descends into the drainage of Big Blue Creek, which, like Lake Fork, drains north to the Gunnison River. Then the road wends through a beautiful, broad grassy swale, brilliant green in early summer, and follows a stream dammed in numerous places by beaver. Bordering this green valley are dark spruce forests.

The road ends at the Forest Service campground.

The mining-camp boomtown of Creede in its heyday (Photo courtesy of Library, The State Historical Society of Colorado)

28

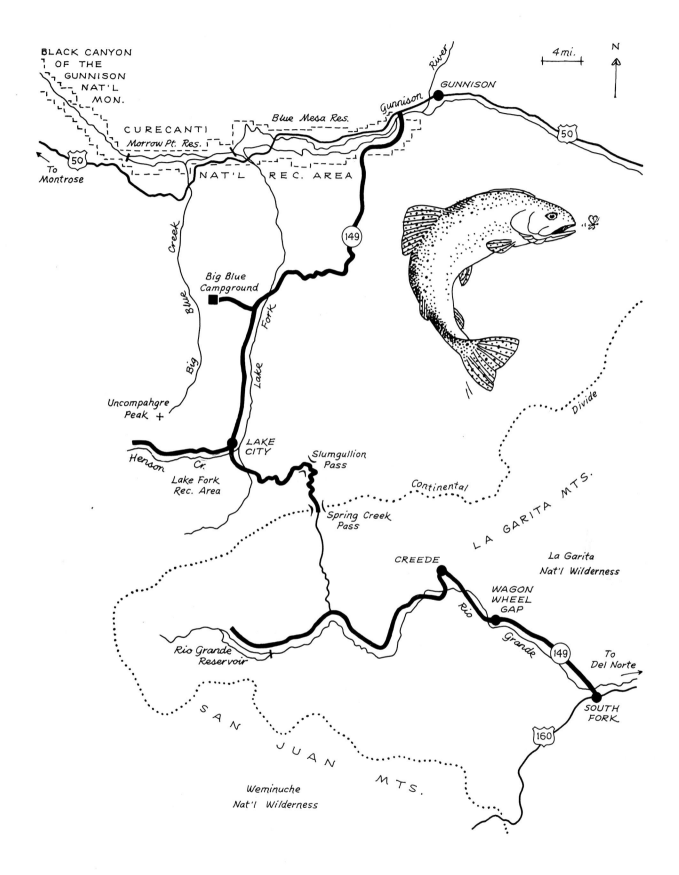

BLACK CANYON OF THE GUNNISON NAT'L MON.

CURECANTI

Blue Mesa Res.

Morrow Pt. Res.

Gunnison River

GUNNISON

50

To Montrose

NAT'L REC. AREA

Big Blue Creek

149

Big Blue Campground

Lake Fork

Uncompahgre Peak +

Henson Cr.

LAKE CITY

Slumgullion Pass

Lake Fork Rec. Area

Spring Creek Pass

Continental

Divide

LA GARITA MTS.

La Garita Nat'l Wilderness

CREEDE

WAGON WHEEL GAP

Rio Grande

149

To Del Norte

Rio Grande Reservoir

SOUTH FORK

160

SAN   JUAN   MTS.

Weminuche Nat'l Wilderness

4 mi. N

50

The headwaters of the Rio Grande, Lake Fork, and Lake City

If you are not in a hurry to backtrack, this is a great place to camp and to explore on foot. The beaver dams alone are worth an afternoon's study, and if you sit alongside one at dusk you may be able to watch some of these industrious rodents going about their work.

Highway 149 continues to Lake City, once the center of considerable mining operations in the area. Today Lake City is best known for the story of Alferd Packer (see "Colorado Sketch: Alferd Packer") and for the many recreational activities available in the nearby Lake Fork Recreation Area.

The road west of town follows Henson Creek and leads to the beginnings of trails into the Big Blue Wilderness Area (formerly the Uncompahgre Primitive Area). In a few miles the road begins to climb steeply and gets pretty rough, making it accessible only to four-wheel drives.

South of Lake City, Highway 149 starts the long climb up the 11,300-foot-high Slumgullion Pass (the name derived from a miner's stew popular in the area at one time). From the top of the pass you get a fantastic view of Colorado's high, wild country. To the northwest, dominating the landscape at an elevation of 14,314 feet, is Uncompahgre Peak. The road descends through thick coniferous forests, then climbs slightly to 10,901-foot-high Spring Creek Pass on the Continental Divide, with superb views of the San Juan Mountains and the Weminuche National Wilderness to the south. You are now in the upper drainage of the Rio Grande, described earlier.

Crested Butte and Gothic

It was a hot summer day when I left Gunnison and headed north on Colorado Highway 135 toward Crested Butte. The land around here begins to look parched and brown in August. The first hay crop has been put up, and the second mowing awaits cutting, flowing in yellow waves before the hot, dry breeze. The simmering highway has quicksilver puddles that disappear as you approach them—heat mirages. You are not aware of it, but the road climbs ever so slowly as you approach the town of Crested Butte, 8,909 feet above sea level. This was my first visit here, and right

The ghost town of Gothic in the Schofield Pass region

Above: *Old cabin in the ghost town of Gothic*
Left: *Abandoned mining building in Gothic*

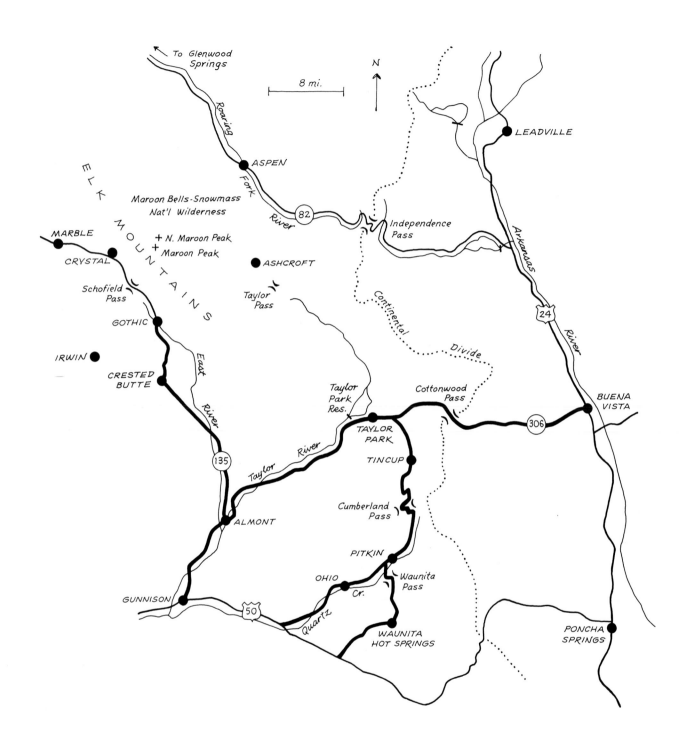

Crested Butte, Gothic, and Cottonwood Pass

away I was struck by the resemblance to the area around Ketchum and Sun Valley in Idaho. Though the sun was still hot, the air here had an exhilarating brace to it.

The mining history of Crested Butte is rather prosaic, for it was coal, not gold, that spurred the establishment of the town in 1879. Within a few years a railroad from Gunnison ran to Crested Butte carrying out the coal from the mines and bringing prospectors into the area. In the early 1880s, gold and silver were discovered in the Elk Mountains to the north, and soon the towns of Aspen, Ashcroft, and Crystal were established. The Elk Mountains form a barrier that prevented easy travel between the Aspen area and Crested Butte, though mule trains did make the trip over high passes that are still accessible only on foot. Today about seventy-one thousand acres of this range are preserved as the Maroon Bells–Snowmass National Wilderness.

I followed the road north from town leading to Gothic. The road winds along a steep hillside, and you can look down into the broad, green valley formed by the East River. Across the valley are Maroon Peak and North Maroon Peak, both, as their names imply, maroon colored. Gothic was a silver mining town with a population of several thousand in the early 1880s. Today only a few buildings remain. General Ulysses S. Grant visited here in the summer of 1880 before the railroad was completed. His party included Colorado's governor, Frederick W. Pitkin, and other state officials, and they traveled by mule team, with the former president doing most of the driving himself (he apparently distrusted anyone else at the reins). Later they headed into the mountains west of here to visit the booming town of Irwin, described later as part of the Kebler Pass trip.

From Gothic the road climbs steeply toward 10,707-foot-high Schofield Pass. You can travel for a way without benefit of four-wheel drive, but eventually it becomes too much for ordinary vehicles, especially if you try to go over the top and down to Crystal and Marble on the other side. However, there are lovely alpine meadows filled with blazing wildflowers not far out of Gothic, and there are any number of places to stop and take in the beauty of the High Country. Incidentally, this is an area where biologists and botanists have been studying various alpine plants to learn how they survive in a harsh climate with such a short growing season.

Cottonwood Pass

If you are in the mood for a reasonably relaxed trip with fine scenery and good camping facilities along the way, this is an excellent choice. Furthermore, if you should decide to stay longer than a day or two, you have the option of roaming several side roads in addition to the main Cottonwood Pass route. In all, the trip could easily be stretched into three or four days of leisurely exploration and camping.

Although at 12,126 feet, Cottonwood Pass ranks among the highest in Colorado, the road to the top is excellent and easily traveled. Take Colorado Highway 306 west out of Buena Vista. This road is paved for the first several miles, then it becomes graveled as it climbs through aspen forests. For the last few miles to the top of the pass, you ascend in wide, sweeping loops above timberline, where there are broad vistas of bare tundra and thick forest below. The summit is on the Continental Divide, and you may wish to stop here to explore some of this land above trees. In most years wildflowers will reach their peak during the first half of August, though some varieties, such as the alpine buttercup, blossom while there is still snow on the ground; it isn't at all uncommon to see the diminutive yellow flowers poking up through the last remaining inches of snow cover.

If you are here early enough in the year, just after the road is open and while snow still lies deep in protected pockets, you may observe the unusual phenomenon known as "pink," or "watermelon," snow. Responsible for this coloration are microscopic algae. Surrounding the chlorophyll centers of the tiny organisms are pink coverings that scientists think protect them from excessive ultraviolet radiation at these high altitudes. These microorganisms can survive in near-freezing temperatures. Incidentally, don't eat any of this watermelon snow. I'm told that it can have a powerful laxative effect on gastrointestinal systems, bringing on an affliction known as the Rocky Mountain Quick Step.

Starting down the west side of Cottonwood Pass, you have distant views of Taylor Park Reservoir and Taylor Park, the latter a mountain-rimmed valley. Before the road was built over Independence Pass north of here, Highway 306 was one of the main supply routes to the mining camps of Aspen and Ashcroft. From Taylor Park the original road headed northwest, then climbed the rugged 12,400-foot-high Taylor Pass

Studying Alpine Plants

The hillside, ablaze with the color of wildflowers, is like a French Impressionist painting run amok. Blue and white columbine, red Indian paintbrush, pink asters, and bright yellow sunflowers all splash their vivid hues across the lush green alpine vegetation. Above it all tower 13,000-foot peaks.

The locale for this scenic splendor is Schofield Pass. Pristine beauty notwithstanding, this is a site for important scientific research. However, it's science with an unusual twist, for some of the investigators are not trained scientists at all. They are volunteers from all walks of life taking part in a program called EarthWatch.

At various times during the summer months, you are likely to see people roaming these hillsides, clipboards in hand, seemingly oblivious to the beauty as they jot down information. If you were to query some of these people you might learn that their professions range from school teachers, lawyers, and truck drivers, to housewives, engineers, or librarians. And they come from all parts of the country. This particular EarthWatch program is under the direction of Dr. David Inouye of the University of Maryland. It's run in conjunction with the Rocky Mountain Biological Laboratory whose headquarters is in Gothic.

The technique of plant study involves laying out a careful grid of nylon twine, stretching scores of feet across a hillside. Within the squares of this grid Dr. Inouye and graduate students make a careful inspection of plant species and density, often calling out cryptic letters and numbers that are recorded by EarthWatch volunteers. Some of the plants have been tagged so growth rates can be studied. The data are often compared to information on computer readout sheets in the hands of the volunteer.

Sometimes a particular plant is the focus of the studies. For example, one such subject is a rather ordinary-looking plant with the scientific name *Frasera speciosa*, also known as green gentian. In recent years these scientific studies have indicated that *Frasera speciosa*, along with certain other alpine plants, may be extremely long-lived—perhaps sixty years or more. This is surprising

EarthWatch volunteers aiding study of alpine plants in the Schofield Pass region

considering the harshness of the climate and the short growing season. Here at Schofield Pass, the deep winter snow may not melt until mid- to late June—and some years fresh snow begins falling in September. Thus the plants may shake off their long dormancy, spread their leaves, blossom, and spread seeds all in a short period of time.

The knowledge gained by these studies is becoming increasingly important because these fragile alpine ecosystems, remote as they may seem, are beginning to experience the impact of acid rain. Moreover, increased recreational use of these high altitude lands is having an impact. In fact, in your own travels here and in other Colorado alpine country, you may well have noticed how off-road vehicles and cattle and sheep grazing have severely affected the plant life. With a better understanding of the plants and animals of these delicate ecosystems, scientists can often make recommendations on how to minimize environmental damage and spare the flora and fauna.

If you visit Schofield Pass in summer and spot some people with clipboards and notebooks, don't disturb them. They are carrying on important research. However, you may stop in Gothic and ask virtually anyone who looks like a resident about the Rocky Mountain Biological Laboratory, where some brochures will give information about the programs. And if you would like to find out how you may volunteer for this and other EarthWatch programs, call 1-800-776-0188.

Opposite: *Colorado's state flower, the columbine, in a high alpine meadow on the road north of Gothic, in the Schofield Pass region*

Above: *Restored building in Tincup, in the Cottonwood Pass region*
Opposite: *Cottonwood Pass road*
Overleaf: *Cottonwood Pass road*

Gas pump and general store in Tincup

Black Canyon: The Backroad Side

Most visitors to Black Canyon of the Gunnison National Monument see this mysterious place from the South Rim, which is easily accessible from U.S. Highway 50. Although the South Rim offers some superb views of this awesome gorge, I prefer the North Rim mainly because it's harder to get to and therefore has fewer travelers. And it really does have the flavor of a true backroad, with meandering curves and lovely country. To savor this place, you should be prepared to spend at least a day and, if you camp, you can stretch this into a few days of leisurely exploration of one of Colorado's most fascinating features.

Get off the main highway, U.S. 50. West of Gunnison and roughly six miles after the highway crosses Blue Mesa Reservoir, watch for the turnoff for Colorado Highway 92 (it's just after the little village of Sapinero). The road crosses the Blue Mesa Dam (one of those dams that probably never should have been built). Once on the north side of the canyon of the Gunnison River, the road climbs and skirts the edge of the gorge. There are several viewpoints where you may pull off and look down into the long, narrow Morrow Point Reservoir (formed by another dam downstream that shouldn't have been built). Although this part of the canyon is spectacular, this is just a prelude to bigger things to come. Gradually leaving the Gunnison River, Highway 92 follows contour lines in and out of valleys formed by creeks that drain from the higher elevations of the West Elk Mountains. At the town of Crawford take the road leading to the north rim of the national monument (the turnoff is well marked). For the first few miles the road is paved, it then turns to a well-maintained gravel road.

If you look east you'll get a glimpse of an unusual geological formation: a volcanic plug. This tower, rising from the valley, was once the throat of an ancient volcano with liquid lava flowing from its conical top. Eventually the molten magma cooled and hardened. Then, over time, the flanks of the volcano, being softer rocks, were eroded away leaving the basaltic plug looking like some modern sculpture.

When you enter the national monument there's a ranger station and, nearby, a lovely campground. Trails here allow you to explore parts of the rim, walking through a forest of gnarled old piñon pines and junipers. The drive along the north rim should be done at a slow pace, for there are numerous viewpoints to explore. At one, The Narrows View, the distance between the rims is actually less than the canyon's

before descending into the Roaring Fork Valley. Even with today's four-wheel drives, the ride over Taylor Pass is rough, slow, and bone jarring.

At the village of Taylor Park, you can continue west, descending into the narrow gorge cut by the Taylor River, to the intersection of Colorado Highway 135 at Almont. To your right is Crested Butte. To the left is Gunnison.

Or, just east of the village of Taylor Park, you can head south to the little town of Tincup (believed to be named after an early miner who panned gold with his tin cup). From Tincup the road climbs steeply over Cumberland Pass (elevation 12,000 feet) before dropping down into the old mining town of Pitkin. Here you can either continue over 10,303-foot-high Waunita Pass to Waunita Hot Springs, or head down Quartz Creek to still another mining town, Ohio. Either way you'll eventually intersect U.S. Highway 50 east of Gunnison. From the time you leave Buena Vista, you have about a dozen U.S. Forest Service campgrounds to choose from along the Cottonwood Pass road, in Taylor Park, the Taylor River canyon, and the Pitkin-Tincup area.

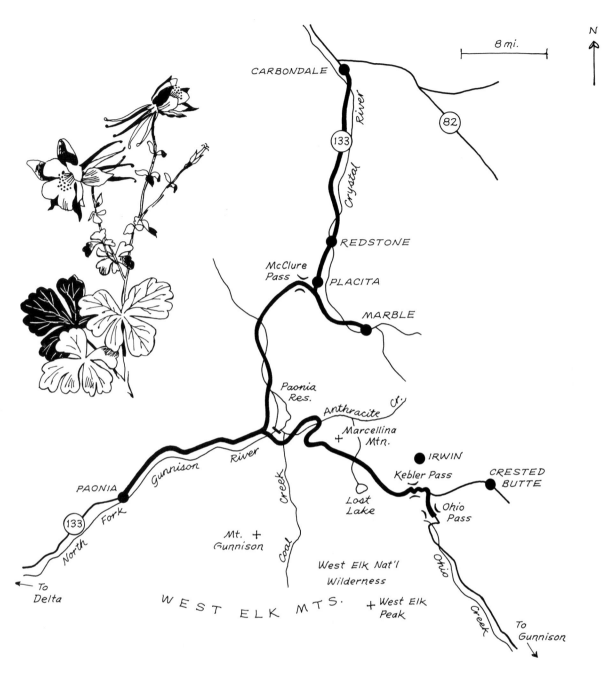

Black Canyon, Paonia, McClure Pass, Kebler Pass, Ohio Pass, Redstone, and Marble

depth—1,150 feet from rim to rim, versus a dizzying, near-vertical plunge of 1,725 feet to the Gunnison River below. These viewpoints and short hiking trails along the rim are definitely not for acrophobics. But they give a splendid look at geological forces at work.

What happened here? Nothing of great and spectacular upheaval. Instead, over two million years, the Gunnison River carved this gorge by the scouring action of mud and silt particles carried by the swift waters. The river first cut through softer volcanic rocks.

Then it encountered hardermetamorphic schists and gneisses that did not yield as readily. But in time the river cut down through them, and the steep walls of the gorge are due to the toughness of these rocks. Peripheral erosion along the canyon edges was much slower than that caused by the swift-flowing Gunnison. And because of these vertical walls, there are deep, dark shadows in parts of the canyon at any time of day, thus the name Black Canyon. Like so many other places, Black Canyon deserves time spent

Above: *Black Canyon of the Gunnison River in the Gunnison National Monument*
Opposite: *Black Canyon of the Gunnison River, from North Rim*

absorbing its beauty.

When you head back out to Crawford (you can't get to the other side from here), you can continue on to beautiful downtown Hotchkiss. Here a left turn takes you to Delta. To the right, the road leads to Paonia.

Paonia to McClure Pass

The town of Paonia is off a little-traveled but lovely road, Colorado Highway 133. It's a good place to start this trip, and the best time is in late summer, for there are numerous orchards and roadside stands that sell the succulent fruits (peaches, apples, apricots, and pears) grown in the valley of the North Fork of the Gunnison River between Paonia and Delta to the west. This is also coal mining country, although many of the mines have closed. You wonder about the incongruity of the dirty mines and a town named for peonies. (It was first called Peonia, but later corrupted by the post office to Paonia.) There is a fine view southeast across this agricultural valley to the West Elk Mountains, with 12,719-foot-high Mount Gunnison the most prominent peak.

Northeast of the town, Highway 133 climbs gradually up past the dam forming Paonia Reservoir. This manmade lake seems to be perennially low, with long mud flats exposed—hardly an invitation for recreational activities. However, as the road heads north beyond the reservoir, it begins to pass through thick aspen forests, and the land takes on a more montane character.

There is a decided Old West flavor to Highway 133 beyond Paonia Reservoir. Several ranches lie in the creek-fed valleys, and the road winds uphill and down, edged with barbed-wire fences held in place by gnarled old posts. Around one of the bends, you are likely to encounter a cowhand urging a herd of cattle along the dusty road.

The last haul up to McClure Pass starts in a dry, dusty valley and goes through several fascinating biological transitions. Along the stream course are cottonwood trees, with sagebrush growing on the hillsides. The elevation here is slightly over 7,000 feet. As the road climbs in slow, winding curves, you enter the zone of Gambel oak, or scrub oak, which have the typical lobed leaves and acorns of the larger species of oak trees, but here grow as dense, tangled stands

rarely over eight to nine feet tall. This tough tangle of brush is sometimes so dense that large animals cannot penetrate it. Scrub oak has always been the curse of the cowboy when calves wandered off into it, for it is virtually impossible to ride a horse through a stand of this oak. Indians were reported to have burned off large areas of it to make travel easier and to provide more browse for deer. But the oak also served the Indians, for they harvested the acorns, and after grinding, baking, and washing them to remove the inherent bitterness, used them in soups and breads. These extensive stands of Gambel oak serve an important biological purpose by providing cover for certain small animals and birds, and their decaying leaves make the soil rich in nutrients, as shown by the frequency of lupine, geranium, mule ears, and other wildflowers here.

Within a few miles of the top of McClure Pass (only 9,500 feet in elevation), you enter the aspen zone, which provides another of those autumn spectaculars. Practically the entire mountainside south of the pass is covered by aspen forests. The transition from scrub oak to aspen marks a difference in precipitation, for although it is low by Colorado standards, the McClure Pass area receives more snow, and retains it longer, than the valleys and hillsides below it.

The descent from here into the Crystal River Valley can be a total riot of color in autumn because of both the foliage and the red sandstone cliffs on the opposite side of the valley. Highway 133 follows the Crystal River north to Redstone and Carbondale, an area covered in the "Redstone and Marble" section.

Kebler and Ohio Passes

This is another tour that begins on Colorado Highway 133, but to the east of Paonia and just before you reach the Paonia Reservoir, you turn right on an un-numbered road leading into the Gunnison National Forest. The road runs along Anthracite Creek for a short distance, then climbs slowly up out of the valley. To the left is 11,348-foot-high Marcellina Mountain, its flanks creased by erosion to give it an awesomely rugged appearance. Incidentally, Marcellina Mountain is within the boundary of the Raggeds Wilderness Area, a little-known mountain region of great beauty. This road, in fact, skirts between two lovely wilderness areas, the Raggeds and the West Elk

Marcellina Mountain in the Ruby Range near Kebler Pass

Above: *Lost Lake near Kebler Pass in the White River National Forest*
Opposite: *West Elk Mountains overlooking Ohio Pass*

Wilderness Area. As the road climbs in elevation, you leave the cottonwood trees of lower elevations far behind, and soon you find yourself in aspen and spruce forests. To the southwest are glimpses of the West Elk Mountains.

This trip is rather special because I discovered one of those delightful jewels of Colorado's High Country, Lost Lake. About ten miles southeast of Highway 133, I followed the U.S. Forest Service signs and turned right on a dirt road. The last mile to the lake can be a bit rough and rutted depending on recent rains, but by taking it slowly almost any vehicle can make it.

The setting is superb: stately old forests of spruce and fir; tranquil lake with excellent fishing; rugged mountain peak rising above as a backdrop. You'll find wildflowers in profusion here in August: Indian paintbrush, penstemon, scarlet gilia, and, of course, the state flower, columbine. The campground at the lake is small and well used despite its relative seclusion. On weekends you may find it filled to capacity. (Be extra cautious about fires, and be sure to leave the campsite spotless.)

As Colorado mountain passes go, Kebler, at about 10,000 feet in elevation, is relatively low. You don't quite get up to timberline, but there are beautiful parklike meadows that invite hiking or picnicking. Just beyond Kebler Pass where a well-marked road to the left leads to Crested Butte, take a sharp right and follow signs to Ohio Pass, a mere thirty-three feet higher than Kebler. Now you're on the old stage road that used to carry passengers from the train depot in Gunnison to such nearby mining towns as Irwin. In 1882, Irwin was a sizable community that boasted two full-time marshals, several hotels, and twenty-three saloons, and was visited by such notables as General Ulysses S. Grant, Theodore Roosevelt, and Wild Bill Hickok. Within a few years Irwin became a ghost town, and its remains can now be visited off the Kebler Pass–Crested Butte road by following the Forest Service signs.

Descending the south side of Ohio Pass, the road switchbacks through extensive aspen forests, making it a spectacular trip in the fall. Most people don't realize that aspen forests grow in such dense stands because they spread principally by shoots from the root system. Sometimes an entire grove can originate from a single tree. Furthermore, aspen are frequently a transitory species in forest evolution, beginning their extensive growth on open or sometimes burned-over areas. Douglas fir and Engelmann spruce are often found growing in stands of aspen because the seedlings of these species require shade provided by the aspen for the first decade or two of their lives. Eventually the conifers crowd out the aspen and become the climax forest.

Only a few miles from the top of Ohio Pass is a thin, silvery waterfall that tumbles a hundred feet or more over a cliff above the right side of the road. There's room to pull off here, and a well-beaten trail leads to the base of the falls. Farther on is the valley of Ohio Creek—broad, open ranch country offering distant views of the jagged West Elk Peak. This road takes you past the remnants of several coal mines and ultimately into Gunnison.

Redstone and Marble

Colorado Highway 133 begins and the Crystal River ends just north of Carbondale. Take the highway here south along the river toward Redstone, situated right across from a long line of old coke ovens. Redstone is a picturesque town with high trees shadowing little Victorian houses, the scene dominated by the tall clock tower of the Dutch-style Redstone Inn. The inn stands at the foot of an aspen- and pine-covered slope.

Today Redstone is a resort, but it was founded in 1902 as a company town, laid out for the miners who worked the local coal mines. John C. Osgood, head of the Colorado Fuel and Iron Company, was shocked by the dilapidated, lice-infested shacks and tents his employees lived in. He planned and built a model village for the workers, with about seventy small houses, different in style and color, as well as a large schoolhouse, a clubhouse, and a firehouse. The inn in those days was the bachelor quarters. Only a few of the original houses are still standing, but many of the newer ones are also Victorian in style.

Of course, Osgood didn't exactly neglect himself. About one mile from Redstone he built a 2.5-million-dollar, forty-two-room Tudor-style manor, which he called Cleveholm. You pass it as you drive down Highway 133. The Redstone Castle, as it is now called, has been completely restored.

For many years I've wondered about the huge marble blocks lying in and along the Crystal River. I know they came from the town of (what else?) Marble, but why so many so far down the river?

Since we first wrote this book back in 1976, we've received from readers many versions of the "true" rea-

The Meaning of Wilderness

I suppose it seems strange to write about the virtues of roadless places in a book about roads, but it makes perfectly good sense if, for no other reason, getting to most wilderness areas requires traveling on backroads.

But the real reason for this short essay is that I've been a strong advocate of wilderness protection for more than three decades of living in the Rockies. Wilderness is a rare and precious commodity. How rare? In Colorado there are a little over 2.6 million acres preserved as officially designated wilderness areas. That may sound like a lot, but it really represents less than 4 percent of the total land area of the state. That's not much, especially in a world shrinking rapidly by modern transportation and burgeoning growth and development.

Colorado's population is growing at an alarming rate. Many of the backroads we write about lovingly here may eventually be paved and widened to accommodate many more vehicles at a faster speed. Rural lands are being subdivided and sold as more people move here. But those preserved wildlands, that 4 percent, is not likely to increase by much, if at all. And so that tiny amount of wilderness must serve us all.

Serve us how? Recreation, of course, is one of the values of wilderness. It's a chance to escape from cars and crowds and to experience some truly pristine country. Hikers, backpackers, mountain climbers, ski tourers, whitewater river enthusiasts, canoeists—all are on the increase. Adventure recreation is the fastest-growing segment of the recreation industry. Physical challenge is a major attraction of wilderness. Of course, as I get older it really becomes a challenge to carry all that damned camera equipment into the boondocks. And I notice these days many more young whippersnappers passing me on the trail. But I don't mind.

Some people talk of the spiritual value of wilderness, a chance to reflect, in quiet and pristine surroundings, about ourselves, perhaps about our origins. I know that when I spend time in wild country my senses come alive, become more finely tuned. I see more, hear more, smell more. Urban life dulls our senses and sensibilities. And I find I can tackle the mundane aspects of everyday life with much more vigor when I return from a wilderness experience.

For purely biological reasons, wilderness is important to us whether we realize it or not. In recent years a new phrase has entered our vocabulary: "biological diversity." Much has been written about the loss of this diversity. And it's true that in the complex web of life on our planet, some of the intricate strands are unraveling. By preserving wild lands we can also preserve some of this biological diversity. "Wilderness," wrote nature writer Nancy Newhall, "may hold answers to questions we have not yet learned how to ask." As a scientist, I couldn't have said it better.

I like to think of it as an ecological savings deposit, an environmental mutual fund, if you will, for the future. Wilderness will only increase in value to us, and future generations will reap its dividends.

For me, Wallace Stegner, one of the West's finest writers, sums it up best: "We simply need that wild country available to us, even if we never do more than drive to its edge and look in. For it can be a means of reassuring ourselves of our sanity as creatures, a part of the geography of hope."

son for these big blocks lying where they are, including: (1) the blocks were dumped by striking miners in 1909; (2) the blocks were carried down to the river by snowslides and washed downriver; (3) the blocks were dumped from railroad cars when the mine was closed in 1941. For all we know, it may be a combination of all of these.

Marble is now a quiet little town, reached by turning left on a gravel road south of Placita and following the Crystal River east for a few miles. Although claims had been staked many years before, there was no great demand for marble until a turn-of-the-century fire in New Jersey showed that it could withstand great heat and so was good for fireproofing buildings. The business boomed, and the town of Marble came into its own. The crowning achievement of the local

Cars of the old Colorado Midland Railway crossing Hell Gate at Hagerman Pass (Photo courtesy of Library, The State Historical Society of Colorado)

mine was quarrying the biggest single piece of marble ever cut; it weighed roughly one hundred tons. By the time it became the Tomb of the Unknown Soldier in Washington, D.C., the huge block had been sculpted down to a little more than sixty tons. The marble for the Lincoln Memorial also came from here. When marble buildings went out of style, the town died. Also, two mudslides that wiped out many of the buildings didn't help. Today relatively few people live here, most of them in the summer.

The cemetery, a short way out of town, naturally has many marble tombstones. On the grave of one young woman, next to the marble stone giving the necessary information, there is a lovely handcarved wooden plaque with just "Karen" on it. Someone loved her a lot.

Hagerman Pass

Curiously enough, the 1926 *Rand McNally Auto Road Atlas* shows the Hagerman Pass route as a state highway. Today the old highway is a backroad, but be forewarned that if your car has low ground clearance, this should be considered a marginal trip—particularly the section at the top of the pass. However, with a moderate amount of clearance or a large amount of luck, the few rough spots can be negotiated. It is well worth the effort, for this is among the most spectacular scenic trips in Colorado, with some fascinating railroad history to boot.

You can start the trip on U.S. Highway 24 just south of Leadville, one of the most famous mining towns on the Western frontier. If you're heading south,

View from the Hagerman Pass road

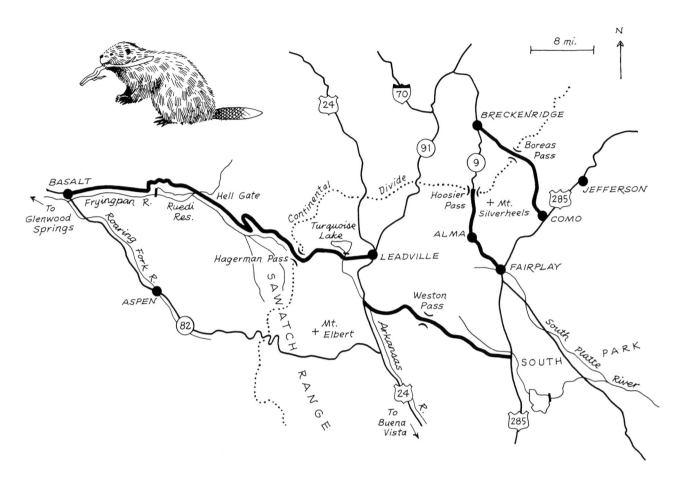

Hagerman Pass, Leadville, Weston Pass, Como, Boreas Pass, Breckenridge, Alma, and Fairplay

take the first road to the right and follow the signs to Turquoise Lake. West of the lake you will climb steadily up an old railbed blasted out of the side of a large, forested canyon. At the head of the gorge, where the road curves to follow the north slope, is the Carlton Tunnel. Today it sits in disrepair with No Trespassing signs plastered on the rusting iron gate that blocks its entrance. At one time, however, the tunnel represented a marvelous feat in railroad engineering.

When the Colorado Midland Railway Company constructed its line from Leadville to Aspen Junction (now Basalt), it had to contend with a formidable barrier, the Sawatch Range. Some of Colorado's most rugged peaks are in this mountain chain, including Mount Elbert, the highest point in the state, with an elevation of 14,433 feet. The railroad followed the most gradual slope up toward Hagerman Pass, but the company opted to build a tunnel at the 11,528-foot

level to alleviate the need for a steep, tough grade over the top. The 2,164-foot-long Hagerman Tunnel, completed in 1888, was not entirely satisfactory. Heavy snows on a steeper-than-normal grade posed problems for the trains.

So in 1890, an independent company that was hoping to profit from tolls blasted the Busk-Ivanhoe Tunnel (now called the Carlton) through almost two miles of solid granite at an elevation almost six hundred feet lower than the Hagerman Tunnel. This new shaft eliminated about seven rail miles. Even though the Colorado Midland paid steep rates to the private company, they were lower than the maintenance costs on the higher route. In 1897, however, new owners of the Colorado Midland sought to save money by reopening the higher and tougher Hagerman Tunnel. The move proved an economic disaster. A bitter winter accompanied by ferocious blizzards closed the line for seventy-eight days, and the company never recovered from the lost revenues in passenger and freight haulage between Aspen and Leadville. Eventually the Busk-Ivanhoe (Carlton) Tunnel was converted to an auto toll road, then abandoned.

Today the Hagerman Tunnel cannot be seen from the present road, but in the vicinity of the Carlton Tunnel an unmarked trail ascends steep hillsides about six hundred vertical feet to the old tunnel.

Beyond the Carlton Tunnel the road climbs steeply in a series of panoramic switchbacks. Near the expansive open top of Hagerman Pass on the Continental Divide, I had to get a running start to cross a small muddy patch of snow, but I made it.

The road down the west side of the pass gets rough in a few places, with a steep incline, ruts, and rocks to slow down the pace. The views are superb. Below is the alpine basin formed by the upper Fryingpan River. All around are high, snowclad peaks. The road twists gradually downward across flower-dotted tundra and a couple of small streams. In a few miles you enter the Hell Gate area where the old railroad (now the road) was blasted through a precipitous, narrow gorge. In the days when the railroad was in operation, trains used to stop here to allow passengers the opportunity to disembark and look over the edge into the frightening depths of the canyon. It is still a little disconcerting today to peer out the driver's side and see the rusting hulks of a few vehicles that didn't make it, lying mangled on the rocks many hundreds of feet below.

After passing the lovely Ruedi Reservoir, the road enters a canyon of colorful rock formations and eventually emerges at the town of Basalt on Colorado Highway 82, in the Roaring Fork Valley. To the southeast is Aspen, and to the northwest, Glenwood Springs. Despite some tough driving, this is a dazzling trip with an incredible variety of beautiful scenery.

Weston Pass

This road follows the old stage route from the broad, mountain-rimmed valley called South Park to the upper Arkansas Valley near Leadville. In 1879, the Denver, South Park and Pacific Railway was extended south several miles past Fairplay to the short-lived town of Weston. There, supplies were unloaded and passengers disembarked for the rough trip to Leadville by way of 11,900-foot-high Weston Pass. The stage lines did a brisk business, one of them grossing nearly half a million dollars in that one year alone, ferrying passengers and freight from the railhead to California Gulch, site of mining activity in the Leadville region. By 1880, when the Denver and Rio Grande Western Railroad was extended into the Arkansas Valley and up to Leadville, stage and freight traffic over Weston Pass diminished radically.

The route today can be easily reached by turning west off Highway 285 about ten miles south of Fairplay (some signs are posted). The first part of the road traverses the western edge of South Park and climbs gradually. The last few miles to the top of the pass are steep and rocky. Depending on rain and snow conditions, you may find this section of the road seriously rutted, making it difficult, if not impossible, to drive on.

When I was only a mile or so from the top, I stopped to photograph the wildflowers. The open meadows here were lush green, and near a spring I found beautiful blue columbines growing in profusion—a rather unusual phenomenon, or so I thought, for most columbines seem to prefer the shade of forests.

At the top of the pass are the remains of some old structures, perhaps part of a mining operation or, more likely, a way station for the stage lines. The only building to survive intact is a lonely old outhouse.

Starting down the west side of the pass, the road becomes rough and rutted again, but gradually it smoothes out and winds down into a wooded canyon where it follows a stream. Beavers have been at work here. The dams they've built have created terraces of ponds over nearly a half-mile stretch. Aspen, a favored food of beavers (they eat the succulent inner bark as well as the leaves and shoots), has been cut and dragged a long distance to serve as building materials for these mammalian engineers.

After almost giving up hope of finding a suitable camping spot, I found an idyllic place in a small meadow next to the stream. By climbing a hillside nearby, I was rewarded with a superb view of Mount Elbert and the Sawatch Range. It was near sunset, and the breakup of a storm over the distant mountains produced an incredible play of light, shadow, and color on Colorado's highest peak.

The next morning, I emerged from this steep little

canyon, drove over rolling hills in the Arkansas Valley, and came to U.S. Highway 24. To the left is Buena Vista, and about nine miles to the right is Leadville.

Como to Boreas Pass and Breckenridge

Boreas Pass on the Continental Divide used to be one of the most feared mountain passes in Colorado. Swept by ferocious winds and storms (Boreas was the Greek god of the north wind), the road up to the 11,482-foot-high pass climbed steeply in sharp switchbacks, seeming to cling "to the edge of eternity," as a frontier poet put it.

In spite of the dangers involved, the Boreas Pass road was a major stage route leading from Como in South Park to Breckenridge. Later, the narrow-gauge Denver, South Park and Pacific Railway was extended over the pass, becoming, for a time, the highest railroad in the country. There's a story told about the Barnum Circus train getting stuck here three miles from the top. Common sense saved the day: The elephants were let out of their cars and made to push the train the rest of the way.

Today Boreas Pass is reached by turning north off Highway 285 midway between Jefferson and Fairplay. In less than a mile, you come to the almost deserted town of Como, marked by the large stone ruins of a railroad roundhouse. Como was a railroad town named after Italy's Lake Como by homesick Italian coal miners who worked the mines nearby. When founded, it was built entirely of tents, the better to pick up and move to Leadville when the railroad construction crews moved on. When the trains no longer came through South Park, the town's population dwindled to the few people it now has.

A dirt road northwest of town follows the old Denver, South Park and Pacific roadbed to the pass. Within the last twenty years, the Army Corps of Engineers stationed at Fort Carson dredged the railroad route and converted it for automobiles. There's a marker along the way in memory of a soldier who was killed while on duty here.

As you ascend the pass, you'll notice signs of mining activity everywhere: a large tramway, a tall load-

Colorado's highest mountain peak, the 14,433-foot-high Mount Elbert, viewed from the summit of Weston Pass

The Leadville Ice Palace

An active mining town is a pretty ugly thing. Leadville in its heyday was no exception. Huge mine dumps, smoke from the many smelters in the valley, and hillsides denuded for fuel left much to be desired in the beauty department. After the repeal of the Sherman Silver Purchase Act in 1893 brought an end to silver mining in the vicinity, reclamation and civic beautification were the last things on Leadville's collective mind. Unemployment and economic disaster were the first things.

So it comes as somewhat of a surprise to learn that in the midst of all this ugliness a structure of great and unusual beauty was built, the Leadville Ice Palace.

The Ice Palace began as a plan for bringing much needed tourist dollars into the town. Tourist schemes were not new to the state: Pueblo had its Mineral Palace in 1890, and every town and city had mini-festivals of one kind or another. Leadville, with its lengthy winters, seemed ideal for a monumental ice structure—its climate has been described as "ten months winter and two months mighty-late fall." The same railroad that used to carry silver out of the town could bring in tourists from Denver. Why, it would undoubtedly bring in people from all over the world, and each and every one of them would be loaded with money to spend in Leadville.

Work on the palace was started in November 1895, with a target opening date of Christmas. This wasn't a small undertaking: The palace turned out to be the largest ice structure ever built in the United States, maybe in the world. When the people of Leadville dreamed, they dreamed big. The site occupied five acres. The building itself was longer than a football field and almost twice as wide. The architect, who had built a smaller ice palace in St. Paul, Minnesota, designed a Norman-style castle with octagonal, ninety-foot-high towers flanking the entrance.

By the first week of December, the wooden interior had been finished and excellent progress was being made on the five-foot-thick outside ice walls. Then the grandiose plans almost went, literally, down the drain. An unheard-of mid-winter thaw brought fifty to sixty degrees Fahrenheit daytime temperatures for almost three

The magnificent Leadville Ice Palace of 1896
(Photo courtesy of Library, The State Historical Society of Colorado)

weeks. About the only things that saved the structure were the below-freezing nighttime temperatures and ten thousand yards of canvas draped over the ice during the day. When the thaw broke just before Christmas and the temperature went back to its customary frigid state, construction was behind schedule. On December 30, the workmen broke all their previous records, but there was still some work to be finished when the Leadville ice palace was opened with much fanfare on January 1, 1896. The town's merchants had given their clerks a half day off, and the miners had been given a day off (without pay, of course) to attend the parade and opening speeches. All of Leadville lined up to pay the fifty-cent admission fee.

And what of all those hordes of expected Denverites and world citizens who would spend mightily to see such a wonder? Well, they came, all right, clutching sack lunches, but not in droves. They saw the amazing structure with its sixteen-thousand-square-foot skating rink and two ballrooms, looked over the exhibits frozen in the inside walls, and left on the afternoon train. The whole endeavor was a financial bust.

By mid-February, Leadville was sick of ice-skating and tobogganing and rock-drilling contests. The weather turned unseasonably warm the first of March and stayed warm. There was nothing to do but close the palace down. The official ceremonies putting an end to the venture were held on March 28.

It had been a grand idea, beautifully executed. Nature and the Denverites just hadn't cooperated.

ing device, many buildings. On the summit is an old log section house left over from the days of the railroad. This building has now been restored and sits resplendently on the summit as it did when the railroad was in its glory. Several dedicated groups made this restoration possible including the Colorado Historical Society, Summit County Historical Society, Como Civic Association, Park County Government, Texas A&M University College of Architecture, Colorado Department of Transportation, Pike and San Isabel National Forests, Harris Construction, and the Ghost Town Club. Hats off to all.

On your way down the other side of the Divide, you'll come to Baker's Tank, a way station that supplied the trains with water from 1882 to 1937. Baker's Tank has been preserved by the U.S. Forest Service. Nearby, the deforested hillsides serve as another reminder of the railroads and the mining operations in the area.

The road continues on to Breckenridge, now a popular ski resort. It started out as a mining camp and was named after U.S. Vice-President John C. Breckinridge in the hopes of getting a post office through his political influence. It worked. A couple of years later, the townspeople were incensed to learn that Breckinridge's sympathies lay with the Confederate States, so they changed the town name to Breck*en*ridge. (That'll show him!) By the way, if you're in Breckenridge at the right time of the year, you can say you've been out of the United States. Three days out of every August, the town is declared a "no man's land." It seems that the area was overlooked in the official process that led to Colorado's becoming a state in 1876, and when the city fathers of Breckenridge finally "consented" to join the Union—which they did in 1936—the town reserved the right to be a "free and independent kingdom for three days each year."

Alma and Fairplay

South of Breckenridge, Colorado Highway 9 crosses the Continental Divide over Hoosier Pass (elevation 11,541 feet). South of the pass, at its foot, lies the town of Alma. It was in this vicinity that the legend of Silver Heels sprang up.

Silver Heels was the name the miners gave to the beautiful dance hall girl who came to the area about 1861. When tragedy struck in the form of a smallpox epidemic, a frantic message was sent to Denver for help, but few persons were willing to come or able to nurse the dying miners. Silver Heels went from cabin to cabin helping in any way she could, bringing food here, comforting a sick man there. Then she too came down with the horrible disease. Gradually, the sickness waned, and the grateful miners raised some $5,000 to present to their heroine. She was nowhere to be found. Did she disappear because she was terribly scarred? Did she go off somewhere to die? Mount Silverheels behind Fairplay is named in her honor.

The little cemetery in Alma, where many of the smallpox victims were buried, can be reached by taking Park County 8 opposite the Alma post office. Follow this route to the Buckskin Cemetery sign, then double back on the dirt road to the right.

Buckskin Cemetery is a lovely place, set in a grove of aspen and evergreens. Wildflowers grow in between and on top of the graves. Many of them have iron or wooden fences around them (to keep out the wild animals—a chilling thought). The whole history of the area can be read on the tombstones: many babies who didn't make it to their first birthdays, whole families dead in some epidemic, a mother and her newborn baby buried together, a man who went out to visit his mine in a snowstorm and wasn't found until June. Death was a real part of these people's lives. Maybe because of that, there's a feeling about this cemetery that the dead should have a beautiful, natural setting in which to spend eternity, a feeling that is lacking in modern, well-manicured memorial parks.

Highway 9 follows the South Platte River from Alma to Fairplay. Along the way, you'll notice large dredging piles, where the riverbed was scooped up, sifted for gold, and then dumped. In this environmentally conscious age, it's hard to conceive of dredging operations being not only tolerated but actually encouraged. It's understandable, however, when you realize that any kind of mining operation meant a town would live and not fade away as so many others had. It didn't matter that the ugly, scarring dredging was at the edge of the town itself. Fairplay didn't fade away, obviously, and today is the county seat of Park County.

Incidentally, when the town was nothing but a group of log cabins, one of the prospectors declared himself the boss and proclaimed "fairplay" for everyone. This early politician later became a notorious highwayman. Times haven't changed much.

Fairplay has done a good job of preserving its his-

Overleaf: *Sunset colors reflected on thunderclouds near Weston Pass*

Prunes, a Burro

They could be stubborn, they weren't very sweet smelling, and they were certainly loud. The first Colorado miner to call burros "Rocky Mountain Canaries" had probably spent many a sleepless night listening to the harsh high-pitched braying of his four-legged companion. But when gold was discovered in the state, the burro turned out to be the perfect beast of burden for the prospectors who began tramping all over the High Country in search of the yellow metal.

Strong and reliable, this small donkey was the ideal pack animal. He could carry his owner; he could carry his owner's mining tools and personal gear; and if his owner was lucky enough to find it, he could carry out the gold.

The burro's surefootedness was indispensable on steep mountain slopes. In emergencies, he could go for long periods of time without food or water, but if there was water to be found, his keen nose would sniff it out. He had an uncanny knack of getting himself and his owner out of tight predicaments. No wonder a prospector valued a good burro.

Prunes was more than a good burro. Prunes was one of the best.

Rupert M. Sherwood needed a burro, now that he was going into the prospecting business full time. He'd heard that a miner who was retiring had an experienced "canary" for sale. The burro had worked the mines in Alma and Fairplay. Twelve years old, in the prime of life. The owner wanted ten bucks for him.

Rupe looked the little brown animal over thoroughly. The burro seemed strong and healthy enough, his teeth were good, he seemed bright and alert.

"You can't go wrong," the owner said.

"What's his name?" Rupe asked as he handed over the ten dollars.

"Prunes," was the answer.

Rupe eyed the burro's shaggy form. "It figures," he said.

Rupe and Prunes were well suited to each other, and a strong bond developed between man and animal. The two of them were soon partners.

The burro's role went beyond that of the typical pack animal. The ever-dependable Prunes could be trusted to run errands by himself. He would find his way down the trail and into a town, mosey over to the general store, wait for the written order he carried to be filled and the supplies loaded on his back, then tote them up to camp.

Rupe and Prunes worked all over the Alma and Fairplay areas, sometimes prospecting on their own, sometimes hiring out to one of the big mining companies. Rupe never did get rich, but he made enough to take care of the two of them and even managed to put aside something for his old age.

Old age did come to both of them. As the years went by, Rupe's aching bones bothered him more and more, but not from the hard work of prospecting—that just loosened him up, made him feel alive. No, it was those windy Fairplay winters he couldn't stand. The city comforts and warmth of Denver began to look pretty tempting to the prospector.

But what about Prunes? There was no way Rupe could take him to Denver for the winter, and he couldn't bear to sell his companion of almost fifty years. Why, it would be like selling his own brother. But Prunes was too old to be just turned out to fend for himself. Still, that appeared to be the only answer to the problem.

Rupe soon found that he didn't have to worry about Prunes's well-being. The inhabitants of Fairplay considered him to be something of a town institution and took over the responsibility of feeding him during the long winters.

Rupe returned to Fairplay in the summers, and he and Prunes would spend the few warm months together. Then Rupe would go to Denver when the weather turned cold, and Prunes would once again resume his daily treks up and down the streets of Fairplay, stopping at each house to get a handout.

Prunes was sixty-three when he died in 1930. He was buried on Front Street, in the heart of Fairplay. Beside his grave the townspeople erected a monument of stone and concrete. But this wasn't your everyday monument—that wouldn't have done justice to the faithful Prunes.

His tombstone is surmounted by a bronze plaque, with the image of the little burro in bas-relief. At the sides are display cases holding newspaper articles about him and his master. The entire monument is decorated with samples of ore from all the mines that Prunes once served. The inscription reads: "Prunes. A Burro. 1967–1930. Fairplay. Alma. All mines in this district." Originally this was spelled out in colored marbles.

Rupe Sherwood died the next year, at the age of eighty-one. In accordance with his last wish, his ashes were buried at the base of Prunes's monument. An iron fence, ornamented with Rupe's mining tools, surrounds the two graves. Rupe and Prunes just hated to be apart.

The townspeople of Fairplay haven't forgotten Prunes and the other "canaries" that worked the mines in the area. Every year, on the last full weekend of July, they stage the twenty-three-mile World's Championship Pack Burro Race along a course over Mosquito Pass. An eye-catching bumper sticker—"Get Your Ass up the Pass"—helps advertise the event. The burros are fitted with regulation pack saddles, loaded with twenty-five-pound weights, and decorated with old-time gold mining equipment. Then they are pulled or cajoled over the 13,188-foot-high pass. The owners are not allowed to ride or prod the burrows but may carry them (none has done this so far) or tug at them with a fifteen-foot-long lead rope. To date, the record time for the round-trip event is 2 hours, 50 minutes, 46.5 seconds. A parade, dance, barbecue, melodrama, and turkey shoot are part of the weekend activities.

Prunes, the ever-dependable burro

Horses and cattle grazing near Hoosier Pass

tory. There are many reconstructed old houses—from log cabins to ornate Victorian buildings—in the South Park City Museum, a restored mining village on the outskirts of town. Many of the buildings were moved here from nearby ghost towns but some are on their original sites. This is not your typical tourist-trap, "reconstructed" Old West town. The museum owes its existence to a farsighted group of South Park citizens who were determined to preserve the area's historic buildings. Volunteers laid the foundations of the first relocated buildings in 1857, and forty thousand items were donated for furnishing the village.

Today there are over thirty original buildings in South Park City. To me, the most interesting is the Stagecoach Inn, moved here from Mosquito Pass. It served as a halfway house from 1879 to 1890, providing a place to stay overnight and a hot meal for miners going to and from Leadville. Travelers ate downstairs and slept dormitory-style upstairs in this small, crude log building—a shack by today's standards. Makes you realize how far accommodations have come along Colorado's backroads.

On Fairplay's main street, you'll notice a most unusual monument. This was erected by the towns-

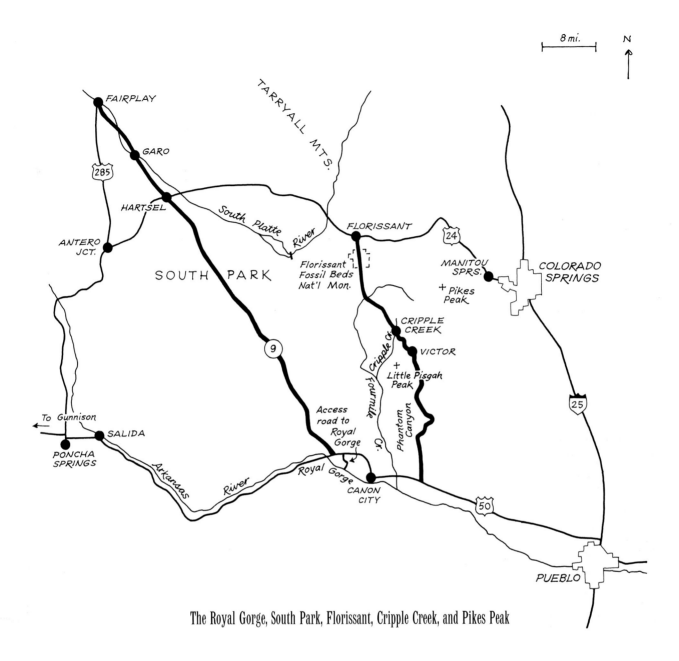

The Royal Gorge, South Park, Florissant, Cripple Creek, and Pikes Peak

people over the grave of one of their premier "citizens" (see "Colorado Sketch: Prunes, a Burro"), the inspiration for a yearly race that draws spectators from miles around.

The Royal Gorge to South Park

A tour of the Royal Gorge—the incredible canyon carved by the Arkansas River—hardly qualifies as a backroad trip because of its proximity to U.S. Highway 50, a heavily traveled route from Pueblo to Salida, Gunnison, and points west. Nonetheless, this one-thousand-foot-deep defile (in places only thirty feet wide) is a popular tourist attraction and you will undoubtedly want to visit it if you are in the area. About eight miles west of Canon City on U.S. 50 is the access road to the gorge.

A mile or so west of the Royal Gorge turnoff on U.S. 50 begins Colorado Highway 9. Although it does not have the most beautiful mountain scenery in Colorado, this route is a pleasant and somewhat different approach to Colorado's mountain-rimmed jewel, South Park. Turning right (northwest) onto Highway 9, you wind between low piñon- and juni-

Above: *Tombstone in the Buckskin Cemetery for twenty-seven-day-old George Morden*
Opposite: *Tombstone in the old Buckskin Cemetery near Alma for Thomas Faley, who was lost in a snowstorm in 1888*

per-covered hills for several miles and climb gradually in elevation. So subtle is the gradient that you only become aware of the change in elevation by noting that the piñon and juniper community is replaced by open, grass-covered hillsides. Ranches dot these hills, and white-faced Herefords graze along the road. The total gain in altitude from U.S. 50 to Fairplay in the northwest corner of South Park is approximately 4,000 feet.

After passing through a small segment of the Pike National Forest, you enter the valley called South Park. This high, broad, grassy basin (it's roughly forty miles long by thirty wide) was first visited as early as 1803 by a Kentucky trapper, James Purcell, who claimed to have found gold here. In 1806, the Zebulon Pike expedition entered the valley over a route paralleling Highway 9 from the vicinity of the Royal Gorge. For the next two decades, the valley was visited by occasional fur trappers in search of beaver. John Charles Frémont reported finding large herds of buffalo and other game (presumably elk and deer) in South Park when he traversed it on his way to Cali-

Right: *Lost Creek near the Lost Creek Wilderness Area in the South Park region*
Below: *Sunset over South Park*
Opposite: *Rainbow over South Park ranch after a summer thunderstorm*

fornia in 1844.

This area was long a traditional hunting ground for the Utes, and even certain Plains Indians migrated here seasonally for the hunt. Traditionally, much of the buffalo meat was cut into strips and "jerked," or cured by drying in the sun. Pemmican—basically a mixture of powdered dried meat and fat with berries and other ingredients sometimes added—was a valuable and nutritious food for the Native Americans when traveling in regions where game was sparse. The mountain men, or fur trappers of the time, adopted it as an important food source during their far-ranging journeys.

In the years following Colorado's first gold discoveries, South Park was an important route to the various strikes. The area itself had some significant deposits of the yellow metal along the South Platte River near Fairplay and Alma and in the Tarryall region north of the valley. In 1879, when the Denver, South Park and Pacific Railway entered South Park from the northeast, the valley became a shipping and transportation center, serving the various mining districts to the west.

South Park is one of those special places in Colorado. The valley today has numerous large ranches. In my travels, I've found few places to match it for scenic beauty. As a photographer, I especially appre-

Above: Ranch along the Tarryall Road in the South Park region
Left: *Thunderstorm over South Park*

ciate the interplay here of storms, clouds, lightning, mountains, and soft, lovely land. There seems to be a never-ending variety of photographic possibilities. I once chased a rainbow for several miles between Fairplay and Red Hill Pass, finally capturing it on film as it arched above a small farm. Sunsets and sunrises here seem to have special quality and intensity of color.

The road continues to Hartsel, where it crosses U.S. Highway 24, then passes through Garo (once a way station for the Denver, South Park and Pacific line), and ends near Fairplay at U.S. Highway 285. These last few miles along the South Platte River from Hartsel to Fairplay give you another glimpse of the unpleasant aspects of gold mining. An abandoned dredge sits in the river channel amid spoil piles of boulders and gravel. It seems likely that this segment of the South Platte will not recover from the damage for a long time.

Florissant and Cripple Creek

Southwest of Pikes Peak, along a rocky little stream known as Cripple Creek, lies one of the most famous gold fields in the world, the Cripple Creek Gold District. A worthless-looking six-square-mile plateau in the crater of an extinct volcano, it has yielded more than $430 million of the precious metal since the 1890s—more than any other single gold deposit ever found. At one time, however, no one would believe there was gold here.

Compared to other gold strikes in Colorado, the Cripple Creek boom started late. The discovery of gold was delayed by a hoax. It all started in 1884 when two prospectors, apparently at the urging of some business-hungry merchants of Canon City, "salted" a vein of rock in the Cripple Creek area. This rock with its falsely loaded gold assayed at a fabulously rich $2,000 per ton, and news of its discovery immediately precipitated a rush to what was called the Mount Pisgah Gold Field (named for the prominent volcanic peak nearby). After a month of feverish digging, the hoax became apparent, and the thousands who had flocked here left in disgust. The incident left a tainted image of the area in the minds of other prospectors, and for the next half-dozen years, few bothered to check into the possibility of real gold in the region.

When a local rancher and cowpoke, Bob Womack, made the first discovery of gold, he had a credibility problem. Besides the bad image left by the Mount Pisgah hoax, Womack—dubbed "Crazy Bob" locally—had a reputation for being unstable and un-

The 14,110-foot-high Pikes Peak viewed from a Rampart Range road

Stagecoaches at the halfway house in Cripple Creek (Photo courtesy of Library, The State Historical Society of Colorado)

reliable. Thus, little credence was given his 1890 strike at first, even after assays showed the ore to be worth $250 per ton, a moderately good value in those days. Gradually, however, word of gold spread, and by 1891 the boom was on. Like many other prospectors of the time, Womack died broke; he had gotten rip-snorting drunk and sold his claim for $500. Over the next several decades, the Cripple Creek Gold District produced an estimated $400 million worth of the glittering metal and made millionaires of almost thirty men.

Mining towns are often associated with famous people, and Cripple Creek is no exception. Lowell Thomas spent his early years here. Jack Johnson, the first black heavyweight champion of the world, was a bouncer in a local saloon, and Jack Dempsey worked in one of the mines.

To me, the most scenic route leading to the town of Cripple Creek is through Florissant Fossil Beds National Monument. From U.S. Highway 24 west of Colorado Springs, turn off at the town of Florissant (French for "flowering" or "blooming") and head south. About a mile from U.S. 24, you enter the national monument, and about two miles farther is the Visitor Center.

This area was the subject of a conservation controversy in the 1960s when some fossil beds here were threatened by land development schemes. In 1969, Congress established the national monument to preserve these paleontological treasures. A stop at the Visitor Center is vital if you hope to understand the significance of the place, for on display are rare, delicate, and exquisitely beautiful fossilized remains of insects and plants that were trapped by spewing volcanic ash and lava flows thirty-five million years ago. The fossils provide valuable scientific information about life forms in the Oligocene epoch. There are also some petrified sequoia stumps in the monument (the largest an astonishing thirteen feet in diameter and forty-two feet in circumference), reached by a short hike from the Visitor Center.

The road climbs gradually as you continue south, then descends into the basin where Cripple Creek is

The Pikes Peak Hill Climb

It was 1916. Americans were enthralled with Mary Pickford, embroiled in a presidential election, and reading Booth Tarkington's bestseller *Seventeen*. They were also in love with the automobile. Thanks to Henry Ford and his $320 tin lizzie, almost four million Americans now owned a car. It was no longer a rich person's toy.

The popularity of the automobile hadn't escaped the notice of Spencer Penrose of Colorado Springs. Always one to keep an eye open for any profitable enterprise, he had already begun to formulate plans for a surefire money maker. "Why not," he postulated, "build a toll road up Pikes Peak?" So what if there was already a cog railroad going to the top? Tourists would be willing to shell out plenty for the privilege of driving their own cars to the summit.

He applied to the Department of Agriculture for a permit and franchise. "Might be pretty expensive," he was told. "The road might cost you as much as $25,000."

"That's no problem. I've got the money," he said. "Shouldn't be too hard. We'll just follow the old carriage road."

One year and $250,000 later, the road to the summit of Pikes Peak was finished.

"Well," said Penrose, "it cost a bit more than I thought, and we still have to compete with the cog railroad. Guess we'd better do a little advertising to start the money rolling in."

Penrose was never one to do anything halfway. His idea of a "little advertising" was to organize one of the most spectacular auto races of the decade, the Pikes Peak Hill Climb.

The Pikes Peak auto race captured the imagination of the country. Driving to the summit was one thing: two cars had already done that, long before the road was built, a Locomobile in 1901 and a Buick Bearcat in 1913. But racing to the top when a wrong move could mean plunging over the side of the mountain into some deep abyss, now that was exciting. It was better than the Indianapolis 500.

Penrose made sure the public's interest remained high by signing up Barney Oldfield, the first man to go a mile a minute on an oval track, as a contestant. If anybody could bring in the crowds, it would be this auto-racing hero.

The hill climb was actually several races, run

Pikes Peak carriage road before the days of the automobile (Photo courtesy of Library, The State Historical Society of Colorado)

over two days. The cars were classified according to weight and engine displacement. The thousands of spectators who lined the road that first day, August 11, 1916, were there not only for the races, but also for the chance to view the most magnificent sports cars of the day. In addition to the Lexingtons, Packards, Dodges, Stutzes, Hudsons, and Chevrolets, were a Rolls-Royce and a Duesenberg. Oldfield was driving a $30,000 French Dèlage and was the crowd's favorite.

Then they were off—literally in a cloud of dust. Around those hairpin curves, skidding on the steep grades, the cars raced the twelve miles to the finish line. And when the first day's racing was over, the winner and champion was Fred Junk in a Chalmers. And when the second day's racing was over, the winner was Ray Lentz in a Romano. Barney Oldfield did no better than twelfth. The altitude had affected his car.

In spite of the embarrassing defeat of its favorite, the crowd proclaimed the Pikes Peak Hill Climb a huge success, and it became an annual event. Today, the auto race from Manitou Springs to the summit and back is held annually in July, and a marathon foot race along the same route is staged every summer.

As for the road, it too was a success, although it wasn't as profitable as Penrose would have wished. And it turned out to be expensive to maintain. When Penrose's franchise ran out in 1936, he shed no tears. For one thing, he was much too busy running the Pikes Peak Cog Railway, which he'd bought when he saw how financially successful it could become. (The train still makes several trips a day out of Manitou Springs in the summer.) Spencer Penrose always did know how to turn a tidy profit.

Above: *Phantom Canyon road from Cripple Creek to Canon City*
Opposite: *Old building near Cumberland Pass*

located. Devastated by a couple of major fires, the community not only survived but somehow managed to retain much of its turn-of-the-century boomtown flavor until recently. It once boasted some forty assay offices, fourteen newspapers, seventy saloons, and a notorious red-light district, Myers Avenue. Two electric trolleys served the area. Like Central City (described in "Black Hawk and Central City"), the Cripple Creek region today is a major tourist attraction.

Although it is backroads country today, Cripple Creek is definitely not a ghost town. Moreover, the town has suffered the same fate as Central City and Black Hawk: gambling joints, heavy traffic, and hordes of people who care nothing about the town's history. You may want to hurry on through. In fact, considering the lack of parking, you may have no choice.

Continuing south, the road leads to Victor, another boomtown, which had several famous gold mines nearby, then descends steeply through Phantom Canyon, a magnificent gorge, and follows one of the old railroad routes. The steep, heavily forested walls of the canyon rise high above, making this a

Above: *Old homestead preserved at Florissant Fossil Beds National Monument*
Left: *Petrified tree stump at Florissant Fossil Beds National Monument*

breathtaking trip. It's a slow drive because in several places the road narrows to one lane. Eventually the road emerges from the gorge and travels across dry, open land to intersect U.S. Highway 50 east of Canon City.

The Front and Rampart Ranges

There are numerous roads, old and new, penetrating the Front Range area between Denver and Colorado Springs. Each of them is somewhat different in its history and scenery. Because of their proximity to the heavily populated areas of Denver and Colorado Springs, the Front Range, the easternmost extension of the Rockies, and the Rampart Range, its southern extension, are more extensively visited than any other parts of Colorado. Nevertheless, there are many interesting out-of-the-way places in the region, and you can spend several days exploring them. But be sure to follow the map of this tour, or you may find yourself lost at times in the maze of roads.

One short trip begins in Morrison, west of Denver. From Morrison, Colorado Highway 74 climbs through the lovely, twisting canyon formed by Bear Creek and ends in Evergreen. Between Idledale and Kittredge is the Lair O' The Bear Open Space Park, one of numerous Jefferson County Open Space Parks established in the Front Range area. It's well worthwhile to stop here and spend some time hiking the easy trails. Big, beautiful cottonwood trees line Bear Creek and the hillsides range in vegetation from mountain mahogany to spruce and pines.

Less well known is the route that leads southwest from U.S. Highway 285 at Pine Junction, located just southwest of Conifer. The road descends into the little town of Pine, but before you get there, you may want to take the turnoff to Pine Valley Ranch Open Space Park. This is another of Jefferson County's Open Space Parks created in recent years. About eight hundred acres in size, the park has numerous hiking trails and picnic shelters. Not long ago, the old ranch house was a marvelous restaurant—in fact one of the finest in the Front Range area. But apparently its remoteness hurt business, and the building is now unused.

Turning left in Pine, which is on the North Fork of the South Platte River, you can follow a narrow, twisting road through the village of Sphinx Park, nestled among smoothly polished granite walls and great monoliths that rise abruptly from the deep can-

yon. This is really spectacular geology, almost a mini Yosemite with the smooth granite walls.

Continuing south on the main road a few miles past Pine, you come to the town of Buffalo Creek. If time allows, you should visit the Green Mercantile, a genuine old country store—the very antithesis of a modern supermarket—housed in a massive granite block building northwest of town. It has been run by three generations of the same family since 1883. Buffalo Creek, incidentally, lies along the route of the old Denver, South Park and Pacific Railway. In fact, just behind the Green Mercantile is part of the old railbed.

At Buffalo Creek, you have several options. You can turn left (north) and follow the road to Foxton, gradually climbing up Kennedy Gulch to join U.S. 285 again just south of Conifer. Or you can follow the road a short way past Buffalo Creek, to the right, which climbs hills and dips into forested valleys, then loops to the northwest to emerge at U.S. 285 in the town of Bailey.

Your third choice is to drive straight ahead about fifteen miles to the town of Deckers, situated on the main branch of the South Platte River. There are spectacular views along this stretch: jagged granite peaks, the plains beyond, thickly forested canyons. There are also many U.S. Forest Service campgrounds and picnic areas to choose from. Deckers was once a popular vacation spot for wealthy Denver families in the days before autos and interstates and ski resorts. The setting here is pleasant indeed. But it was almost destroyed.

It was called Two Forks Dam, an ill-conceived project for storing water by means of a massive dam that would have inundated Deckers and backed water up nearly to Pine. What would have been lost were marvelous free-flowing stretches of the South Platte and the North Fork of the South Platte Rivers, both considered prime trout fishing streams and both in the heart of scenic, forested canyons. Fortunately, concerned citizens rallied to stop the dam. At public hearings conducted by the U.S. Army Corps of Engineers, hundreds of people spoke out overwhelmingly against the project. Good sense finally prevailed and the project was dropped. For now. Someday in the future, however, it may be resurrected if Denver continues to emulate Los Angeles in its uncontrolled growth.

The road intersects Colorado Highway 67 at Deckers. To the left the highway follows the South Platte River for a short distance, then continuing

Overleaf: *The Front Range rising abruptly from the flat plains*

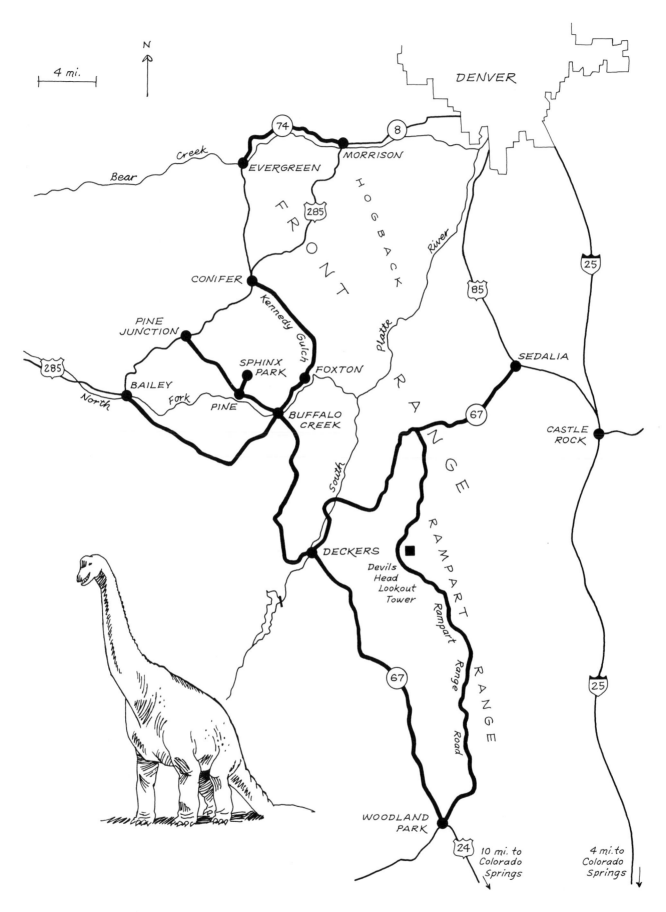

The Front and Rampart Ranges

northeast, climbs steeply out of the canyon and descends to the town of Sedalia on U.S. Highway 85, in the plains. About fourteen miles northeast of Deckers, halfway to Sedalia, you have still another fascinating option, a side trip down the Rampart Range Road. Well marked, this road heads south for almost forty miles before joining U.S. Highway 24 near Woodland Park, northwest of Colorado Springs. Along the way be sure to stop at the Devils Head parking area and take the short hike to the Devils Head fire lookout tower, where there are superb views of Denver and the plains.

Devils Head is another of those places purported to have buried treasure. Here, according to local legend, is $60,000 in gold eagles, the loot from a robbery of a government train in the 1870s. Before they were captured, the robbers buried the money and marked the spot with a knife in a nearby tree. As in most treasure tales, the men never returned to retrieve the gold (some versions of this story allege that they were killed shortly after burying it), and it's still there for the finding.

If you choose to follow Highway 67 to the southeast at Deckers, it will take you through rolling, forested countryside past many farms and ranches. There are magnificent views of Pikes Peak to the south. This road too joins U.S. 24 at Woodland Park.

Empire, Georgetown, and Guanella Pass

Both Empire and Georgetown lie along or near bustling Interstate 70, so technically neither is in backroads country. But you can't always avoid starting a tour on a major road, and besides, you'll miss many interesting places if you do, such as Georgetown, which is also the beginning of a fascinating trip into more remote and scenic country.

However, if you're headed west from Denver on Interstate 70, you'll come to Empire first. Take the turnoff to U.S. Highway 40 and drive two miles to this old mining town. Unlike so many other communities that sprang up where gold was discovered, Empire survived after the mines played out, becoming an important stage and supply station on the Berthoud Pass route over the Continental Divide. And it's still going strong. While you're in Empire, don't fail to visit Peck House, a one-hundred-year-old hotel complete with antiques and brass beds. The restaurant here is excellent.

From Empire, you backtrack to Interstate 70 and then continue southwest to the Georgetown exit. To anyone who has lived in Colorado long enough, the name Georgetown usually evokes images of quaint Victorian homes and buildings. Indeed, this once-booming mining town has some of the finest examples of late–nineteenth-century architecture in the state. Unless you're on an extremely tight schedule, you'll want to spend a while here, exploring the old houses and browsing in some of the shops.

Unfortunately, the character of this charming town is changing. Georgetown citizens voted to build a shopping center of discount stores hardly in keeping with the character of the town. On learning this a friend asked, "Why would anyone move to a rural mountain town and then try to turn it into Denver? If people can't live without shopping malls and discount stores, why not stay in Denver?" Good questions.

In Georgetown, follow the signs in town pointing the way to Guanella Pass. As you start the upgrade to the pass, don't be dismayed by the warning sign "Do Not Overestimate Road Width." (Not me, friend. I have great respect for narrow roads.) After a few switchbacks, you'll come to an overlook with tremendous views of Georgetown and the valley.

The road gains quite rapidly in elevation at first; then it climbs gradually in a series of looping turns. Typically, the character of the forest changes as you approach higher elevations, with the trees assuming gnarled, stunted forms near wind- and snow-raked timberline.

At Guanella Pass itself (elevation 11,669 feet) are broad vistas of tundra and peaks. Immediately to the southeast is Mount Bierstadt, named for the famous nineteenth-century painter of the Western wilderness, Albert Bierstadt. The mountain's 14,060-foot-high summit blocks the view of Mount Evans. To the west are Grays Peak and Mount Wilcox, 14,270 and 13,408 feet in elevation respectively.

To me, the outstanding feature of this trip, in addition to the superlative scenery, is the opportunity of seeing one of Colorado's more unusual forms of wildlife, the white-tailed ptarmigan, or "snow grouse." I suspect that even long-time residents of Colorado know nothing about this bird, usually associated with arctic or semi-arctic climes. The smallest of the grouse family, ptarmigan live above timberline year round. Marvelously adapted to this harsh environment, these birds provide a classic example of protective colora-

Above: *Georgetown*
Opposite: *Split-rail fence near Guanella Pass*

tion. In winter, their plumage and even their eyelids turn completely white to blend with the snow-covered terrain. In summer you are likely to see them in the Guanella Pass region, their white feathers replaced by a mottled gray and brown that blends nicely into the rock-strewn tundra. In fact, as you hike along open expanses above timberline, you may pass several ptarmigan without knowing it. They frequently crouch low to the ground and remain still, allowing you to approach within a few feet. This is especially true in the nesting season, during early summer.

Perhaps your best chance of spotting ptarmigan is to park your car at the top of Guanella Pass and walk east or southeast up the gentle slopes of Mount Bierstadt. Even if you don't see one of these alpine denizens, you'll find this rewarding for the scenery is magnificent and the hike exhilarating.

As the road begins its descent from Guanella Pass, you'll come to several small alpine lakes, then enter forested country again by the former Geneva Basin ski area. Lower down, Geneva Creek parallels the road and races along, foaming white, beneath stately old spruce trees. Eventually, the road intersects U.S. High-

way 285. You can return to the Denver area by turning left. To the right, the highway enters the northern part of South Park via 10,000-foot-high Kenosha Pass.

Black Hawk and Central City: In Memoriam

When *Backroads of Colorado* was first published in 1978, we wrote enthusiastically about Black Hawk and Central City. This region represented an important part of Colorado's colorful history, and a trip to these two towns was certainly worthwhile.

No more.

The sense of history and the charms of the region are gone, replaced with sleazy gambling joints. And Colorado Highway 119, the backroad we once described as being an enjoyable drive, can be extremely hazardous to your health today. The Colorado State Patrol reports a dramatic increase in serious and fatal accidents on that stretch of highway. The reason? High-rolling gamblers hightailing it to and from the gambling joints (with more than a few drunk drivers

The Dinosaur Hunters

A few miles west of Denver, the first foothills of the Rockies rise abruptly from the flat plains in a long ridge known locally as the Hogback. This area is a favorite spot for school field trips because of the abundance of fossils.

I was along with my son's class one day when suddenly a little boy yelled, "I found one! I found one! I found a dinosaur!"

Well, not quite. The small gray rock he held out so proudly for everyone to admire contained the fossilized remains of some long dead plant. But it easily could have been a dinosaur fragment. A bone found in almost this same spot one hundred years ago touched off an era of dinosaur discoveries that unearthed most of the species of these prehistoric creatures we know today.

Dinosaurs, generally, were enormous reptiles with small brains. They lived for 130 million years, then mysteriously died out. When an individual dinosaur died and was covered with sand, silica or other mineral compounds gradually replaced the bone, and the animal turned to stone—became fossilized. The largest of these monsters lived in the Jurassic period, so the rock laid down during this age, the Morrison Formation, yields the fossils of these super dinosaurs.

Now, nobody knew all this in 1877, least of all schoolteacher Arthur Lakes. All he knew was that he found a mighty big vertebra near the town of Morrison, Colorado, while out hunting fossilized leaves. He sent a description of it to paleontologist Othniel Marsh. Marsh's ho-hum reply was that he'd have to see it to identify it. Lakes went back to the Hogback and, sure enough, found more bones. This time, he sent specimens not only to Marsh, but also to another well-known paleontologist, Edmond Cope.

What Lakes didn't realize was that these two eminent scientists were bitter personal and professional enemies, jealous of each other's accomplishments. When they found that the bones they now held belonged to a prehistoric monster fifty to sixty feet long—the largest yet discovered—the scientific fireworks were set off.

Since Marsh had sent Lakes one hundred dollars for the specimens, he could claim the Morrison site. Cope had to relinquish his fossils to Marsh.

The Morrison Formation, however, is extensive. Another schoolteacher, O.W. Lucas, was puttering around in the Morrison Formation near Canon City, Colorado, when he too found some enormous bone fossils. This time, Cope was the beneficiary of the specimens. They turned out to be even larger than the ones Lakes had found. Cope lost no time in getting his crew to the Canon City site.

In 1877, there was still another great dinosaur graveyard discovery. Two railroad men sent Marsh word of an area where bones littered the landscape for seven miles around. The fossil deposits at Como Bluff, Wyoming, were every bit as spectacular as they had said, and Marsh worked the Morrison Formation there for twelve years. It yielded twenty-six new species of Jurassic dinosaurs.

Year after year after year, tons of fossilized bone were dug from these fantastic dinosaur quarries. Both Cope's and Marsh's crew worked summer and winter, always wary for spies from the other camp. The game was find 'em, dig 'em out, and publish before the other one could. Unfortunately, Cope, because of bad financial investments, ran out of money and had to give up the expensive pleasure of dinosaur hunting.

The feud was over. And while most feuds are destructive, this one was not. Two positive things came out of it.

The obvious gain was the vast amount of knowledge gleaned by the scientific community. Before Cope and Marsh began their dinosaur hunt, these prehistoric animals were known only from bits and pieces. Now scientists had hundreds of new species to study, many of them complete skeletons.

The other, more obscure, benefit was the arousal of public interest in these mammoth reptiles, something that had probably never occurred to Cope and Marsh. But there's nothing like the skeleton of an eighty-foot-long, eighty-ton *Brachiosaurus* to fire the imagination. It was this interest that paved the way for the preservation of the great dinosaur deposits discovered by Earl Douglas on the Utah-Colorado border. He would have just laid a claim to his find. Not good enough, said President Woodrow Wilson, and the deposits became part of Dinosaur National Monument when it was established in 1915.

When you think about great feuds of history and literature—Hatfields and McCoys or Capulets and Montagues—add Cope and Marsh. The world was the winner of that one.

The road to Guanella Pass from Georgetown

The restored Georgetown Loop Railroad

as well). It seems that these people have no interest in the scenic or historical values and are only in a hurry to get there (or get home). Even if you make it to either town safely, with all the casino traffic, you're not likely to find a parking place.

It probably won't be long before Highway 119 is "improved," making it fast and easy for the gamblers to get to and from Central City and Black Hawk. All the more reason to stay away. It's a shame that nice places are destroyed by perverted values.

Here's what we wrote about Central City and Black Hawk in the first edition of *Backroads of Colorado*, but keep in mind that you can't experience it in the same way today:

Colorado's gold rush era. This is where it all began. The funny thing is, it was started by a rumor.

Beginning in 1858, there were widely circulating rumors in the Midwest and East of fabulous gold strikes in the Rockies. The prospectors who hadn't cashed in on California's riches a decade earlier hoped to find their bonanza now. By the fall and winter of 1858, the gold seekers began congregating at the confluence of Cherry Creek and the South Platte River, a site soon to become known as Denver. They came by the dozens, then by the hundreds, waiting for the snows to melt in the High Country. They didn't know it, but the rumors were only partially true: What had actually been discovered were small, scattered placer deposits, hardly the stuff of great fortunes. Then in July, like a self-fulfilling prophecy, a rich lode was found in the North Fork of Clear Creek, in the mountains west of Denver, and the gold rush was on.

Even by today's standards, the influx to the region was truly astounding. Within months, an estimated twenty thousand prospectors, entrepreneurs, prostitutes, gamblers, and swindlers flocked to this part of the Front Range, although the harsh mountain winter soon forced many to retreat to the plains of Denver. And after all the surface ore and placer deposits had been scoured, corporations were formed to extract the rich ores by hard-rock underground mining. The area was called the "richest square mile on earth," and it fostered the towns of Central City, Black Hawk, and Nevadaville, among others. In all, it yielded more than $75 million in gold. But gradually, even the big mines folded, and people moved on, following rumors of great strikes elsewhere.

The best place to start on this tour is Golden, where you pick up U.S. Highway 6 as it winds alongside Clear Creek. Once a heavily traveled major route, U.S. 6 has been supplanted in places by Interstate 70

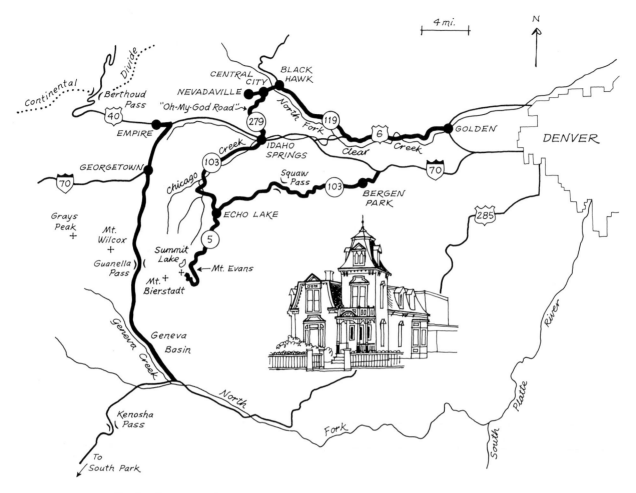

Empire, Georgetown, Guanella Pass, Black Hawk, Central City, Mount Evans, and Squaw Pass

and is now a relatively quiet backroad along this stretch. In about ten miles, the highway branches, and you take Colorado Highway 119 north, following the North Fork of Clear Creek to the old towns of Black Hawk and Central City. On this part of the trip, you can see some of the detrimental aspects of mining, the large dredging piles of lifeless gravel left behind in and alongside the stream.

There is a lot to see in Black Hawk and Central City, and both are thriving tourist attractions. Each of them has numerous back streets and roads leading to old mine sites and tailings piles. Central City has restored such marvelous old buildings as the famous Opera House, once considered the finest theater west of the Mississippi, and the Teller House hotel, with its notorious painting, the *Face on the Barroom Floor*. There are some interesting old tombstones in the Dory Hill Cemetery in Black Hawk, and between the two towns a granite monument marks the spot where John H. Gregory made the first gold-lode discovery in Colorado. A few miles west of Central City is

Nevadaville, formerly a boomtown with a population of several thousand and today a bona fide ghost town.

Extend your trip by continuing south to Idaho Springs, and you'll be driving on what is euphemistically called Colorado Highway 279. This is a well-maintained gravel road, but definitely not suitable for large motor homes and trailers or for acrophobics and the fainthearted. Backtrack to Central City from Nevadaville and follow the signs to Idaho Springs. As the road winds slowly up a hillside, you'll have fine panoramic views of this gold-boom country. For a fee, you can drive in to see the spectacular glory hole, a huge manmade crater, several hundred feet deep and one thousand feet long, from which millions of dollars in ore was extracted. (Note: This is no longer true; the Glory Hole is closed to the public.)

The remainder of the highway down into Idaho Springs is what local residents refer to as the "Oh-My-God Road." You'll quickly understand why, for it twists in tortuous switchbacks down steep hillsides. There are no guardrails, and in places the road is so

90

The "Oh-My-God Road" from Central City to Idaho Springs

narrow that from the passenger-side windows you can see the steep drop-offs. On a white-knuckle scale of one to ten, Highway 279 ranks about eight in places, but the drive provides magnificent views across Clear Creek Canyon to Mount Evans in the distance, and that makes it worthwhile. Adjacent to Interstate 70, Idaho Springs is an interesting old, as well as a modern-day, mining town. There are more than one hundred mines nearby. It's also an old and modern-day tourist resort. The Radium Hot Springs here, which were frequented by the Indians long ago, are still be-

ing used by health seekers.

Mount Evans, Squaw Pass, and Bergen Park

This tour makes an interesting extension of the Central City trip if you take the "Oh-My-God Road" to Idaho Springs. (If you come into Idaho Springs on Interstate 70, take the Mount Evans exit.)

Colorado Highway 103 leaves Idaho Springs and

begins a gradual ascent up the valley formed by Chicago Creek. When nuggets were panned here in the 1860s, this valley, like the Clear Creek Valley to the north, was stampeded by gold seekers. As the road gains in elevation, the character of the forest begins to change. In Clear Creek Canyon around Idaho Springs, the hillsides are dry, and ponderosa pine is the predominant tree species. Not many miles up Chicago Creek, you'll begin to notice mixed stands of spruce and aspen. Higher still are lodgepole-pine forests, and as you approach Echo Lake, which is really not even a hamlet for it has no winter population, the pointed spires of sub-alpine fir become more evident.

At Echo Lake (elevation 10,600 feet) is the beginning of the highest automobile road in the United States, Colorado Highway 5, also known as the Mount Evans road. It's paved and well maintained, but open only in summer and early fall, for obvious reasons. As you begin climbing in ever steeper switchbacks, the forest continues to change. Soon the alpine fir becomes dwarfed and gnarled from the struggle to sur-

Above: *View east from Mount Evans looking toward upper Bear Creek*
Right: *Mountain goat at home above the timberline on 14,246-foot-high Mount Evans*

Gnarled limber pine near the summit of Mount Evans

vive in this hostile environment.

At one of the last turnoffs near timberline, watch for the signs indicating bristlecone pines. These twisted and stunted timberline ancients, found in relatively few places in the world, may be among the oldest living things on earth. Biologists have confirmed that some of them are over four thousand years old.

Leaving behind the last vestige of trees, you are now in the world of alpine tundra. Wildflowers in July and August are spectacular, as are the views from the road down into cirques and into the lake-dotted basins that form the headwaters of Bear Creek to the east. Beyond Summit Lake, the road becomes steeper and narrower. After about twelve miles, you arrive at the top of 14,264-foot-high Mount Evans. All along this road, and at the summit, there are excellent opportunities for short hikes to explore the tundra. If possible, you should allow plenty of time to stop and walk around. Among the common tundra flowers are purple moss campion, blue alpine forget-me-not, yellow paintbrush, yellow and white marsh marigold, and the strange purple blossoms of sky pilot, also known as alpine skunkflower. The latter name is apt, for though the flowers are beautiful, the leaves have a skunklike odor when they are crushed. If you are really ambitious, you might try to get an early start on the Mount Evans road to watch a magnificent sunrise over the eastern plains.

This is mountain goat country. In fact, it's one of the few places in North America where you can see these unusual animals in the wild and at fairly close range. (Sometimes they are actually standing on the road, totally oblivious of cars and people.) Mountain goats are not native to Colorado, and these were introduced to the Mount Evans area by wildlife biologists in the early 1960s. They seem to have done well, and the current herd here numbers well over one hundred. In the summertime, when the Mount Evans road is open, the goats are shedding their long, shaggy winter's fur. These animals are marvelously adapted to their environment, with soft pads on their hooves that aid in climbing steep rock faces that seem all but impossible to scale. They feed year round on the short alpine grasses: In summer the grass is luxuriant and rich in nutrient value, but in winter the goats often have to scratch about in the snow to find enough to eat. Actually, and despite its elevation, parts of Mount Evans have only a thin layer of snow in winter due to the high winds that sweep it away. With their long, thick fur, the goats are well protected against the savage cold. The young are born in the spring, and by the time the Mount Evans road is open (usually in early June), they may be seen gamboling among the rocky boulders and in the alpine meadows above timberline, though never far from mama.

There are also bighorn sheep on Mount Evans. These were native to the region, but the bands on Mount Evans were transplanted from other areas many years ago. Apparently any native bighorns on Mount Evans disappeared decades ago due to hunting and human population pressures. Currently the bighorn sheep of the region are suffering from a serious lung parasite, and many have died. Your chances of seeing one on Mount Evans are not as good as seeing mountain goats, but they can often be spotted.

Back at Echo Lake, Highway 103 leads over 9,807-foot-high Squaw Pass and into the village of Bergen Park. From the pass you can catch glimpses of the "Oh-My-God Road" across the valley of Clear Creek.

Nederland, Allenspark, and Estes Park

Originally we suggested this trip as an extension of the Black Hawk–Central City mini-tour. However, if you're wise you'll avoid the gambling crowds there and start this tour by taking the Golden Gate Canyon road off Highway 93 north of Golden. (This is a much more

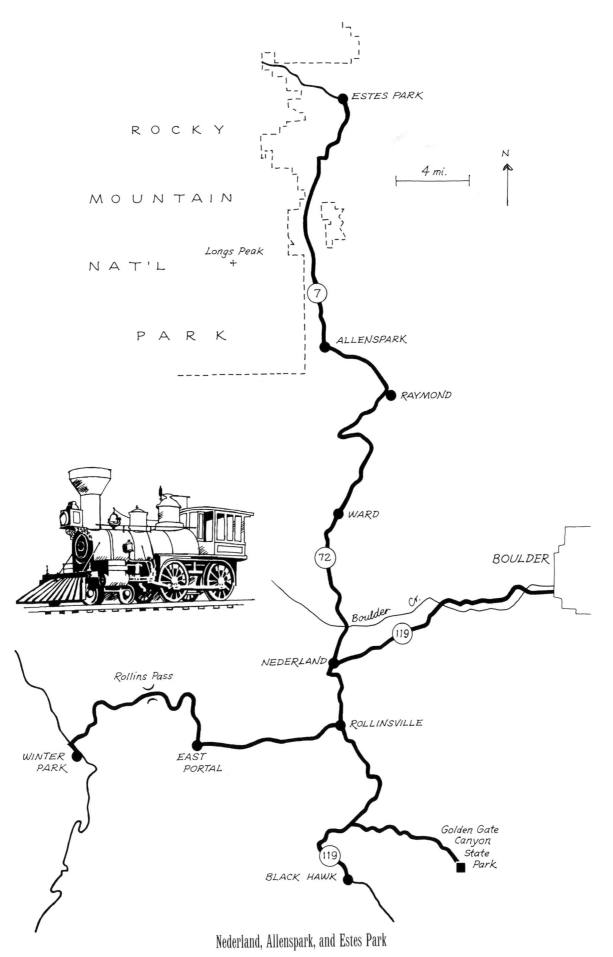

ROCKY

MOUNTAIN

NAT'L

PARK

Longs Peak
+

ESTES PARK

4 mi.

N

⑦

ALLENSPARK

RAYMOND

WARD

⑦²

BOULDER

Boulder Cr.

119

NEDERLAND

Rollins Pass

ROLLINSVILLE

WINTER
PARK

EAST
PORTAL

Golden Gate
Canyon
State
Park

119

BLACK HAWK

Nederland, Allenspark, and Estes Park

scenic route anyway.) After winding through the lovely Golden Gate Canyon State Park, the road intersects Highway 119 north of Black Hawk. This route is my own favorite way to get to Rocky Mountain National Park, but be forewarned that the roads are winding and the driving slow. There are several possibilities for side excursions, and the leisurely pace allows you to savor what, in my opinion, is some of the finest scenery in the Front Range.

Not long after you head north on 119 there's an interesting side excursion that begins in Rollinsville. Take the gravel road left, following signs pointing the way to the village of East Portal. The road parallels the main line of the Denver and Rio Grande Western Railroad. At East Portal is the entrance to a six-mile-long railroad tunnel that cuts under the Continental Divide and emerges near the town of Winter Park. The tunnel replaced the tortuous route over Rollins Pass, now part of the automobile road. The drive over the pass is worthwhile in itself, not only for the scenery but also, if you're a railroad buff, for the marvelous engineering of the wooden railroad trestles. This is an excellent summertime trip if you allow enough time to cross over the Divide to the Winter Park area.

If you backtrack from Rollins Pass or East Portal to Highway 119, you'll continue north through Nederland. The name of this town is derived from the Dutch word meaning "lowland," a seemingly improbable moniker, for Nederland is at an elevation of 8,234 feet. By comparison to the towering mountains west of here, this could, of course, be termed a lowland. Incidentally, those mountains to the west and northwest are an extension of the massive Front Range that comprises Rocky Mountain National Park to the north.

From Nederland, you can take Highway 119 northeast through ruggedly beautiful Boulder Canyon to the city of Boulder or, to continue north, take Colorado Highway 72 through Ward and Raymond, then Highway 7 through Allenspark and eventually to the town of Estes Park, gateway to Rocky Mountain National Park. This portion of the trip is especially scenic and pleasant, with glimpses of Longs Peak, 14,256 feet in elevation, along the way.

A word here about Rocky Mountain National Park. I haven't included a description of the park because, technically, it isn't a backroad area. For one thing, there are enormous numbers of visitors here in

Aspen in full autumn glory in the Rocky Mountain National Park

Isabella L. Bird

When the transcontinental railroad was completed in 1869, and a trip out West didn't consist of months on the trail fighting hunger and thirst, the tourist business in Colorado started to pick up. The state became a favorite spot for the wealthy English, but as tourists, their chief activities seemed to be admiring Western sunsets, shooting buffalo, and sneering at the backward, uncouth natives.

There was one English visitor who was different.

Isabella Bird was a spinster lady of forty-two, traveling alone that September of 1873, when she stopped off in the Colorado Rockies on her way home to England from the Sandwich Islands (now Hawaii). She hated the embryo Western towns and cities. The plains, hot and constantly dusty, bothered her. But the mountains, rising clean and pure in an unending line, were like nothing she had ever seen before, and she loved them passionately.

When someone told her about the mountain resort area called Estes Park, she was determined to visit it. Oh, it wasn't for the likes of her, they said. It was hard to get to; it was almost winter in the High Country, and a noted badman lived up there, practically in the park itself. It took two weeks of trying to find a guide, and at least one abortive attempt to get there, before she finally made it.

Estes Park was worth the effort. The scenery was everything Isabella had imagined; the accommodations, while rustic, were agreeable; and the desperado, Mountain Jim Nugent, wasn't such a bad sort after all.

In fact, she got on so well with him that when he suggested a climb up Longs Peak, she readily agreed. The ascent was grueling. Isabella begged several times to be left behind, only to be patiently cajoled, pleaded with, and finally hauled bodily to the 14,256-foot-high summit by Mountain Jim. It was an amazing accomplishment for a cultured, middle-aged Englishwoman of her day. Longs Peak had first been climbed only five years before her ascent.

Isabella now had two loves: the Rocky Mountains and Mountain Jim. However, the first snows had already fallen, and she knew that if she were to see any more of the Colorado mountains, she'd have to leave Estes Park.

She set out on a six-hundred-mile trip that was to take her south to Colorado Springs, west to South Park, and back north to Denver. She became the first, the original Colorado backroads traveler. Even today, in a car, bad weather can make this a risky trip in November. Isabella did it alone, on horseback, and with no compass. It was an even greater feat than her Longs Peak climb.

There were very few roads as we know them. And she rode through snowstorms and below-zero cold. In places, she had to lead her pony through waist-deep snow. Each night, she faced the same problem: Could she find a house whose occupants would be willing to give room and board to her and her horse? But this didn't seem to bother her. She was glad, she said, that there were so few inns because this way she could meet the people.

And meet them she did—everyone from millionaire cattle barons to desperadoes. At one place where she spent the night, she found out later that the body of a hanged man was still in the tree next to the house.

In spite of the hardships, she was happy. She was surrounded by the magnificent mountains, and that was enough. Well, almost enough.

When she returned to Denver, she didn't stay there long. It was back to Estes Park, almost snowbound by now, and Mountain Jim.

This story of the Englishwoman and the mountain man should end with "And they lived happily ever after in the mountains they both loved." But this isn't a fairy tale.

Jim, it seemed, was subject to drunken sprees and "black moods." He couldn't change and, for that matter, neither could Isabella. She wasn't about to give up her adventurous life to become one of those work-hardened pioneer wives of the West. So that was that.

When she returned to England, she published the story of her Colorado adventures in a book called *A Lady's Life in the Rocky Mountains.* Her

*Believe me
Yours Very Sincerely
Isabella L Bishop*

descriptions of the mountains are eloquent, and her love for them is obvious. She wrote about Jim in a much more restrained manner. Tantalizingly, she gave only hints at their mutual deep affection, but by then she was marrying someone else, someone back home. Even so, that's the way a proper Victorian gentlewoman would write about a love affair, isn't it?

(Photograph and signature courtesy of Library, State Historical Society of Colorado)

Above: *Ranch along a backroad near Radium*
Left: *The Gore Range and the Eagles Nest Wilderness Area,
from Highway 9 along the Blue River Valley*

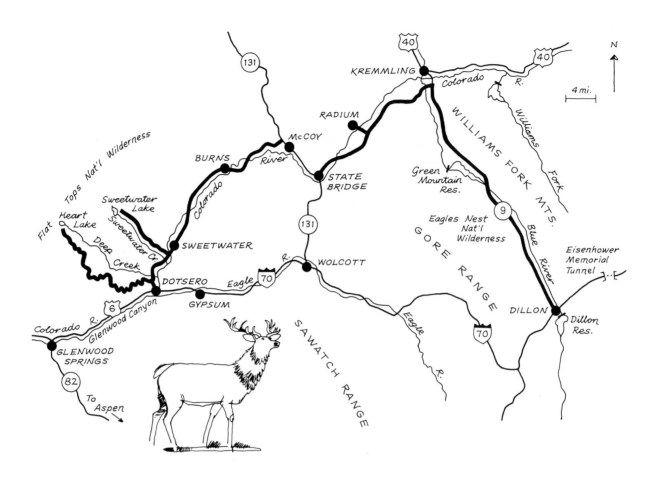

The Blue River Valley, the Road to Radium, the Colorado River, and the Flat Tops

the summertime. However, in keeping with the general theme of seeking out-of-the-way spots, I suggest that you consider sampling the fine hiking trails in the park. Ranging from a few hours to a few days in duration, these hiking trips will take you to little-known but spectacular places. Rangers at park headquarters can advise you on areas to visit, and maps and trail guides are available here. Hiking is a good way to get away from the crowds. Another alternative is to visit the park in September or early October, well past the peak of the tourist season.

The Blue River Valley and the Road to Radium

The first part of the Blue River Valley–Radium trip begins on Colorado Highway 9, which is only marginally a backroad since it is fairly well traveled, especially in the summertime. But the drive is lovely, and it's a convenient way to get to less well known

country in the second part of this tour. After passing through the Eisenhower Memorial Tunnel, Interstate 70 drops steeply down to the town of Dillon, where you take Highway 9 north. The road parallels the Blue River. To the west is the Gore Range, now a part of the Eagles Nest National Wilderness. The Blue River Valley is predominately ranching country. The river itself is a sparkling stream fed by the Dillon Reservoir. There are several places where you can pull off the highway to try your hand with a trout fly.

About two miles south of Kremmling, just before the road dips down to the Colorado River, keep a sharp eye out for a road leading to the left and a sign pointing toward the village of State Bridge. For the first several miles, this road is paved (barely) and climbs open hillsides that give you a fine view of the Blue River Valley, the southern portion of the Gore Range, and the Williams Fork Mountains to the east. The road soon levels out, then begins to descend in winding curves through aspen and spruce forests. At one sharp, final bend there is a magnificent view of the gorge carved by the Colorado River, and a convenient turnoff allows you to stop for a better look. Almost one thousand feet below are the whitewaters of the river. Although here the Colorado is only about fifty miles from its origins in Rocky Mountain National Park, it already has the characteristics of a big, powerful river. The steep gorge upstream is ample evidence.

At this point, the road becomes graveled and is literally carved from the side of a cliff as it descends to the broad valley below. This isn't spectacular country, but because it is off the general tourist routes, it has a quiet charm. Bright sandstone formations add color, and there are elegant old ranches hidden in thick groves of cottonwoods.

I was intrigued by the name Radium, so I took the marked turnoff, followed a dusty road a few miles to the north to the Colorado, and crossed an old steel truss bridge over the river. Radium turned out to be a collection of eight or ten rather nondescript houses, with no sign of a store or a public building and no one wandering around of whom to ask how the village got its name. The road leading north into the hills was marked "Closed," so I didn't try it. There was ample evidence of human habitation here, with cars and pickups parked in front of houses, but not a soul to be seen. I felt as though I had blundered into some calamitous event out of a science fiction movie, the kind in which all the inhabitants of a town have mysteriously disappeared. I retraced my path across the shiny tracks of the Denver and Rio Grande Western Railroad, back across the bridge, then stopped for one last look at Radium. Still no one to be seen. No movement at all across the way. Somewhat later, after doing a little research, I learned that the town was named by a man who thought he'd discovered a radium mine here.

The gravel road continues southwest below colorful sandstone bluffs, then crosses the Colorado about four miles east of State Bridge. At the railroad crossing on the north side of the river, I had to wait for a train to pass—one of those long, long freights that took forever. I was the only person on that road for miles, and I got stopped by train traffic! But the scenery was pleasant, and I went down to throw rocks in the river as the train crept by.

The road continues southwest and joins Colorado Highway 131 at State Bridge. From here, it more closely parallels the Colorado. The mini-tour along this stretch of the river is described next.

Along the Colorado River

There's a tendency to forget that the Colorado River has its origins in this state. To many people, the river seems more closely associated with the spectacular canyon country of Arizona and Utah than it does with Colorado. But there are more than just traces of the Grand Canyon's character here where the river is still young—not only the stretch between Kremmling and State Bridge (just described) but also west of there, between McCoy and Dotsero.

I had been intending to explore the road from McCoy to Dotsero for years, but I always seemed to be in too much of a hurry on my way to or from somewhere. So there was delicious anticipation when I turned off Colorado Highway 131 a mile or so north of McCoy and followed the signs pointing the way to Burns. Right off I discovered that this is unusual country. For being so close to the high central mountains of Colorado, the area is surprisingly mild and almost desertlike in character, making it a great place to visit in the fall. At any other time of year, there is color enough from the sandstone hills and cliffs along the river. But when the golden hues have gone from the heart of the High Country, the aspen, cottonwoods, and willows here are just reaching their peak.

South of Burns, the valley closes in and the canyon walls rise high above the river, the road, and the railroad (the Denver and Rio Grande Western Railroad tracks run along the river also). There is a little resort with log cabins (there used to be a restaurant) at Sweetwater. Instead of continuing south, you can take a short, restful side trip just beyond the town. Make a right turn on a road that runs along Sweetwater Creek. It leads west to Sweetwater Lake and a lovely campground in the White River National Forest. South of Sweetwater, the canyon really gets steep and rugged, with pine forests providing a beautiful contrast to the maroon-colored sandstone cliffs. The road ends at Dotsero and Interstate 70 just east of the spot where the Colorado River has carved Glenwood Canyon.

The Flat Tops

Shortly after setting out on this trip, I knew it was going to be special. About two miles north of Dotsero, I turned off the paved road and headed west along the bottom of a steep, narrow canyon formed by Deep Creek. The cottonwoods were at their peak of autumn

Above: *Colorado River near Burns*
Opposite: *Bridge at Radium spanning the Colorado River*

color, tempting me to stop and camp (it was already late afternoon), but I kept on and soon began to climb steeply in a series of tight switchbacks. I drove steadily upward for almost an hour, as the sun sank below the horizon, and it seemed as though the road would never level out. In places, it is a long, long way down over that edge of road. Finally, in the twilight of early evening, I reached a plateau and pulled off into a secluded aspen grove. I cooked supper and sipped a cup of wine while watching the soft amber alpenglow on

the mountains to the southeast toward Aspen. Lights glowed in the deep blue shadows of the Eagle River Valley below. The spectacle was made even more superb when a full moon rose out of the Sawatch Range to the southeast. I took a late night stroll through the faintly lit aspen before turning in.

The next morning was crisp and clear. A light frost lay on the grass as the sunlight slanted through the aspen. I was sitting in the back doorway of the van, sipping my first cup of coffee and enjoying the peace-

Above: *Horses grazing along the Colorado River near Burns*
Opposite: *Deep Creek Canyon on the road to Heart Lake in the Flat Top Mountains of the White River National Forest*

ful scene, when suddenly I heard a noise to my left in the woods. I turned to see a huge bull elk—sleek, fully antlered, and in his prime—edging cautiously toward me about fifty yards away. His breath steamed from his nostrils in the cold air. Unfortunately, the movement of my head was enough to spook him and he trotted off rapidly through the aspen with his nose held high and his antlers thrown back to clear the brush. Naturally I didn't have a camera within quick reach. He was gone in a second.

Later I discovered that I had only begun to explore this marvelous road. It winds on for many more miles through vast open country interspersed with groves of aspen and patches of subalpine fir. The average elevation here is about 10,000 feet. I'm told that there is an old ghost town known as Carbonate in the area

somewhere north of Glenwood Springs. I didn't find it, but I did spot numerous mule deer at the edge of the road. There is an awesome view of upper Deep Creek, an immense, colorful gorge that is somewhat reminiscent of Utah's Cedar Breaks country. Finally the road ends a few miles beyond Heart Lake, and from here there are trails into the Flat Tops National Wilderness, a 102,124-acre preserve of mountains, rolling hills, forested river valleys, and grassy parks in the White River and Routt National Forests. (The Flat Tops are named for an abrupt outcropping of lava in the center of the region.) Because this is a dead-end road, you can have the pleasure of savoring it again on the way out.

Magnificent country. I strongly recommend that you allow at least a day, if not two days, to enjoy it fully.

Part II
The Western Slopes

▲▲▲▲▲

Technically speaking, the Western Slopes begin on the western side of the Continental Divide and thus include a portion of the Rocky Mountain country covered earlier. But because much of the plateau region has a longer traveling season than the high mountain areas, I've limited the Western Slopes section to approximately the western third of the state.

The Western Slope country has a different character from the other parts of the state. This is a land of transition between the high alpine peaks of Colorado and the great sandstone and desert country of Utah and Arizona. Dominating features are plateaus, mesas, canyons. The farther west you go, the more arid the land becomes. Instead of cool green forests, you find red and orange sandstone formations, sagebrush, cactus, and junipers.

The Colorado Plateau region is actually a series of 4,000- to 8,000-foot-high plateaus separated by steep-walled canyons. There are mountain ranges in this area also. In fact, a number of Colorado's highest peaks of more than 14,000 feet are found here, in the San Juan and San Miguel Mountains. To me the appeal of this part of Colorado is the enormous variety of landforms and vegetation. Within hours, you can sample alpine tundra, forests, desert, as well as canyons and mesas. Here, too, are some of the state's wildest rivers: the Colorado, the Dolores, the Gunnison, the Green, and the Yampa. The canyons of the Gunnison, Green, and Yampa are among the world's most spectacular.

San Juan Range from Cascade Divide Road in the Durango region

For those interested in archaeology or paleontology, the Western Slopes region is a paradise. Near Four Corners, the only point in the United States that is common to four states, places such as Hovenweep National Monument and Mesa Verde National Park offer glimpses into the lives of some of the region's earliest inhabitants, the pre-Columbian ancestors of the present-day Pueblos. It's a fascinating world, and one that should be explored at a leisurely pace.

At Dinosaur National Monument, two-thirds of which is in Colorado, you can see the fossilized bones of such prehistoric reptiles as *Stegosaurus* and *Brachiosaurus,* the latter ranked as the largest land animal of all time, with a height of forty feet and a

Left: *Courthouse Mountain viewed from the road near the summit of Owl Creek Pass*
Overleaf: *View from the Buford–New Castle road*

weight of eighty tons. The monument contains the largest deposit of fossilized dinosaur bones anywhere. A visit here provides an insight into Mesozoic and Paleozoic times. And for a look at stark, beautiful geological processes, there is Colorado National Monument.

The prime features of some of the Western Slopes country for the backroads buff are the generally mild climate and the possibilities for a relatively early and late driving season. Beginning in April, when Colorado's High Country is still locked in the icy grip of winter, you may find it possible to travel many of the backroads in the Western Slopes. You should, of course, check locally about road conditions before taking off. And be apprised of long-range weather forecasts. There's always the chance of being snowed in somewhere during a spring storm unless you heed warnings of impending weather changes.

Fall comes late here. Sometimes fall lasts for several weeks, from late September to mid-October, between the peak of autumn color in the High Country and the height of fall in the milder Western Slopes. It's also well past the regular tourist season, so you'll find places quiet and unused.

Along the Williams Fork

I won't pretend that this is Colorado's most scenic country. It isn't. But it has a pleasing flavor all its own, even if there are no 14,000-foot-high snowcaps in evidence.

I really don't know what made me decide to take this trip along the Williams Fork. Perhaps I was intrigued by the little dot on my map that represented a place called Pagoda. A name like that in itself tends to pique the curiosity. I mean, a lot of Colorado place names reflect the rugged life out here in the early days. Troublesome. Cripple Creek. Fort Wicked. Battle Mountain. Cannibal Plateau. Some names, such as Ouray, Arikaree, Uncompahgre, and Saguache, are direct loans from the Native Americans; others, such as San Luis, Cortez, and Monte Vista, came from the Spanish. Still others, such as Silverton, Telluride, Granite, and Basalt, reflect the mineral wealth or geology of the sate. But Pagoda?

Well, I had to take a look for myself. I had visions of an exotic Oriental temple, or a facsimile thereof, stuck out here in the middle of nowhere. So I left the town of Craig and followed Colorado Highway 394 south and east for about five miles, and then headed straight south on a gravel road. After climbing gradually over some low hills, I descended into the valley of the Williams Fork. Although it was early summer, the scrub oak leaves already looked parched from the heat.

The Williams Fork is a lovely stream whose origins lie in the Flat Tops to the south of here. Along the broad valley are several ranches, one of which seemed a curious combination of Old South and Old West—a huge, two-story log mansion with white-painted balustrade and porch.

When my road intersected Colorado Highway 317, also graveled, I turned left and made a rough estimate from my map of the remaining distance to Pagoda. Just five miles.

Tooling along in a cloud of dust, I must have lost track of time and mileage. Suddenly, flashing past in a blur, something caught my eye. I hit the brakes and skidded to a stop in a spray of gravel and dirt, then backed up. There it was, a boarded-up, broken-windowed old store with a peeling sign—"Pagoda." Well, so much for my illusion of finding an ornate temple. There wasn't a clue as to the origin of the exotic name.

I drove on past the turnoff for the road that heads south to the Flat Tops and the White River. In a little canyon, I rounded a bend and saw one of those sheepherder wagons, with a horse tied nearby. I stopped for a picture. When I climbed back into the van, I heard the insistent, unmistakable hissing of a tire going flat. Damn. The road was pretty narrow, and even though I hadn't seen a car yet, I was nervous about changing a tire here. So I continued on, climbing up out of the draw, and stopped on a broad level stretch of road.

As I was finishing my tire-changing chore, a beat-up old pickup truck came roaring out of the canyon and slammed to a stop. When the cloud of dust settled, the old-timer at the wheel asked if he could be of some help. I thanked him and pointed out that I was doing fine, then asked him about Pagoda. "Named for a mountain peak," he said. "Back there toward the Flat Tops country." Ah well, there went my final chance for some colorful history.

The last miles of this trip are decidedly unscenic, for there is a huge coal strip mine near the town of Oak Creek. I thought about backtracking and taking that road to the south toward the White River, but prudence got the better of me. I turned left on Colorado Highway 131 and headed toward Steamboat Springs to get my tire fixed.

Incidentally, don't confuse the Williams Fork

Williams Fork Valley ranch house in a style combining the Old South and the Rocky Mountain frontier

here, which is a branch of the Yampa River, with the Williams Fork of the Colorado. And yes, speaking of place names, there are two Williams Fork Mountains in Colorado. The range in this area, though, hardly compares with the one in the High Country.

The Elk River Valley

Steamboat Springs has become a popular resort destination, both in winter and summer. It's a lovely locale, but an even lovelier place is located about twenty miles north, the Elk River Valley.

The thing I like about the Elk River Valley is its relative peacefulness. Even in the peak of tourist season, few people venture here. That may be because it's not on the main route to anywhere. You can head north into Wyoming, but it's only on winding, twisting Forest Service roads, and you'd better know where you're going. (But then, that's even better for die-hard backroaders. Getting lost is half the fun.)

At the north end of Steamboat Springs, take County Road 129, following signs to the airport. Continuing north past the airport turnoff, the road winds through lovely ranch country and, for a way, follows alongside the cottonwood-lined Elk River. The valley is quite wide and to the west are low hills, while northwest are the Elkhead Mountains. In late summer it's haying season, and the ranches along the road have bailed or rolled hay in the fields, preparing for the long winter season.

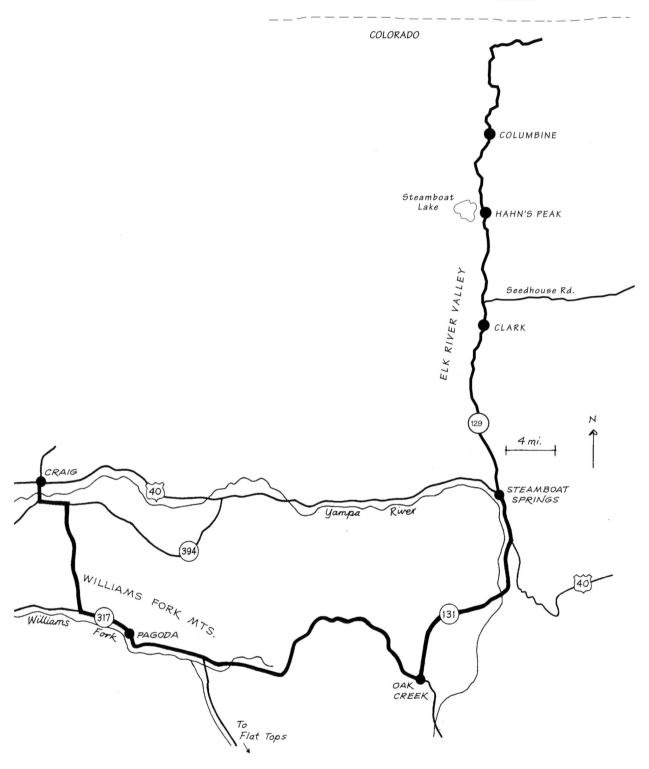

The Williams Fork and the Elk River Valley

Above: *All that remains to identify the town that was once Pagoda, in the Williams River Valley*
Left: *Sheepherder's covered wagon and horse along the Williams Fork Valley*
Overleaf: *Seedhouse Road and the Mount Zirkel Wilderness Area in the Elk River Valley*

Old cabin in the ghost town of Columbine north of Steamboat Springs

About eighteen miles north of Steamboat is beautiful downtown Clark. The town of Clark consists of a general store, a liquor store, and a post office, all in one delightful old building. That's it. But then, what more do you need? The Clark Store sells gas, has a good selection of groceries (and some great beef jerky), and the best wine selection I've seen in western Colorado! It's true. You can buy here some of the finest cabernet sauvignons or chardonnays available, along with some rather nice champagnes and cognacs. And you may want to do just that. I can't think of a better way to enjoy one of those warm autumn days than to have a leisurely picnic lunch with a chilled chardonnay under some fluttering, gold aspens along the Elk River. Why such a wine selection for discerning tastes in an out of the way place? Well, it all has to do with Ken Jones and the Home Ranch (see "Colorado Sketch: Ken Jones, Renaissance Cowboy").

A little north of the Clark Store is the turnoff (on the right) for Home Ranch. About a half mile beyond that you cross the Elk River and here you have a choice: To the right is the Seedhouse Road; straight ahead, Highway 129 heads toward Steamboat Lake and the old ghost towns of Hahn's Peak and Colum-

bine, eventually crossing obscurely into Wyoming. Either choice is great; in fact, you should plan to explore both options.

Continuing north on 129, the road climbs past hillsides thick with aspens (a great trip for fall foliage) before leveling out in a broad valley with a great view of Hahn's Peak, the almost perfectly cone-shaped mountain to the northeast. Be sure to stop at the little town of Hahn's Peak. There are a few interesting little stores here, and most all of the buildings are the originals built in the gold-mining days around the turn of the century.

Steamboat Lake is an interesting side trip, although being a manmade reservoir and subject to water-level fluctuations, the shoreline is often rather stark and sterile. Much more interesting on other side roads are some small natural lakes tucked away in the forest. One of these is Pearl Lake, the turnoff to which is a few miles before you reach the town of Hahn's Peak. It's a pleasant spot for a picnic and the fishing is great. Incidentally, there's a road around the west side of Steamboat Lake that eventually returns to Clark, passing though some pleasant ranch country and along the eastern base of Sand Mountain (named

Boarded-up cabin in Columbine

for its white, eroded flanks).

Several miles north of the town of Hahn's Peak is a little collection of cabins known as Columbine, another former mining town. From here you can head north to the Wyoming border, but in the region are numerous Forest Service roads that can provide some interesting explorations.

Back near Clark, the Seedhouse Road, mentioned earlier, is one of my favorites. It's only about twelve miles long and dead ends at the trailhead for the Mount Zirkel Wilderness Area. But it's such a delightful trip that some years, in autumn, I've averaged two rolls of film to the mile. About six miles in, on the right side, there's a spot where the Elk River has carved a small gorge. It used to be a Forest Service picnic area, but some big boulders now block vehicle access (just as well, because it's a delicate place). If you park on the road, it's only a one-hundred-yard walk to the edge of the gorge. There's a small waterfall as well. A great place to spend an afternoon (or morning or whole day) watching dippers, or water ouzels, catching insects along the stream.

At the end of the road, a trail leads into the Wilderness Area. In a half mile the trail divides; one fork leads to Pitkin Lake, the other to Gold Creek Lake. Either one is a worthy trip, although you should allow a full day for either so as not to hurry it. On the Gold Creek Lake portion there's a side trail leading to a spectacular little waterfall, Gold Creek Falls.

Browns Park and the Gates of Lodore

This trip takes you into the desolate northwest corner of the state, a rugged area carved into deep canyons by the Green and Yampa Rivers. At the town of Maybell, turn off U.S. Highway 40 and follow Colorado Highway 318 northwest. Before doing so, however, check your gas supply, for it's a long way to the next service station.

In about nine miles, you will cross the broad, sleek Yampa River near Sunbeam. From here north, the land is open and dry, with hills covered by junipers, sagebrush, and piñon pine.

This stunted and gnarled species of piñon pine was once an important food source for the Native Americans. Each fall, the women and children gathered the small, sweet pine nuts in straw baskets.

119

Above: *Rolled hay and ranch in the Elk River Valley near Steamboat Springs*
Left: *Fluorescent aspen leaves against an early September snow in the Elk River Valley*

Home Ranch and Ken Jones, Renaissance Cowboy

He's a songwriter, a musician, a poet, a cowboy, a humorist, a conservationist, a world traveler, and the owner and founder of one of the most successful ranch resorts in America. Ken Jones was born in Texas but spent most of his early years on the Hualapai Reservation on the south rim of the Grand Canyon. Later the family moved to Montana where his father owns a cattle ranch. Throughout his teenage years, Ken spent summers as a wrangler on a dude ranch near Cody, Wyoming, a job which undoubtedly helped shape his ideas for a truly unique ranch resort.

In the late 1970s, Ken and a partner bought several hundred acres of land bordering the Elk River near Clark. And almost immediately, he began construction of a new dude ranch. But this was no ordinary resort. The main lodge and cabins were constructed of huge logs, and the design had to meet Ken's stringent criteria of energy efficiency and aesthetics. Guest cabins were placed carefully in some aspen groves and situated in such a way as to minimize any damage to the lovely forest. As a result of this careful work, Home Ranch has become a showcase of impeccable design. In addition to their exterior beauty, the main lodge and cabins feature antiques and artwork selected by Ken and his wife, Cile.

The ranch opened its doors for guests in January 1980 and became an almost instant success. At first its winter trade was greater than that in the summer by virtue of Ken's plans to make it a premier destination for cross-country skiers. With dozens of miles of superb trails winding through forest and over foothills, the ranch attracts cross-country skiers from around the world.

In a relatively short time span, Home Ranch has become a world-renowned destination for winter and summer travel. It is one of only a handful of American resorts to be listed in the prestigious *Relais et Chateaux* international directory. Major stories about it have appeared in *Time, Condé Nast's Traveler, Travel & Leisure, Town & Country, Bon Appétit, House and Garden, Outside*, and many major national and international newspapers.

Much of the ranch's success stems from its food, perhaps among the finest cuisine available anywhere in the United States. The chef, Clyde Nelson, trained under one of the few master chefs in America and worked and studied in notable European restaurants.

Ever in search of new challenges, Ken Jones also pursues his life-long love of music. He's a self-taught musician and guitar player, and is good enough to play onstage with Willie Nelson at Farm Aid 7 and with Roy Rogers and Dale Evans at the 1994 Western Music Festival. He and his band, Cowboy Ken and the Ranch Hand Band, have produced an album, *Campfire Songs*.

Wearing yet another cowboy hat, Ken is actively engaged in environmental work to save the beauty of the Elk River Valley. Working with other ranchers, he is making a concerted effort to put large land holdings in a conservation easement to help prevent massive and destructive land developments that have claimed so many other rural areas in Colorado. The success is evident: The Elk River Valley remains one of the unspoiled jewels of rural Colorado.

If you'd like to stay at Home Ranch, make your plans well ahead of time. The ranch is often booked a year in advance!

Home Ranch in Elk River Valley near Steamboat Springs

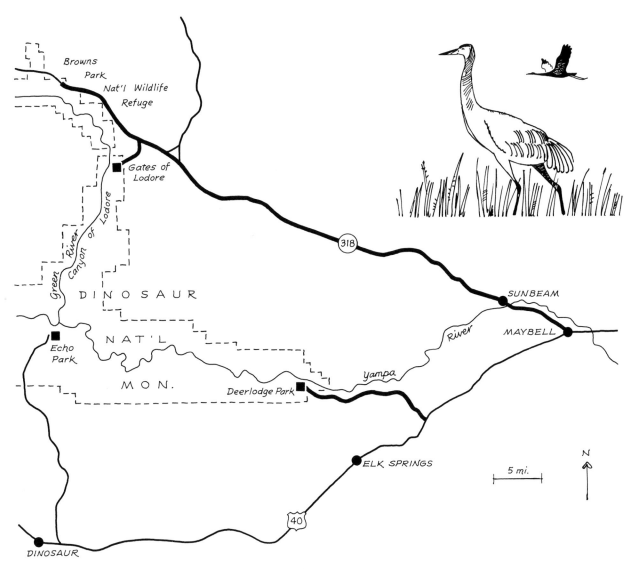

Browns Park, the Gates of Lodore, and Deerlodge Park

Whenever I'm in piñon country in the fall, I gather some myself, if the squirrels and jays haven't beaten me to them. You may have to settle for a sample, because it takes patience to consume any reasonable quantity. The small, hard shell must be cracked with the teeth before the sweet meat can be extracted. Someone once questioned whether a person could survive in the wilderness on piñon nuts alone, considering their tiny size and the time and energy required to extract the nutritious meat.

About sixty miles from Maybell is a side road, marked by National Park Service signs, that leads into the northernmost tip of Dinosaur National Monument. If you follow this road, you come down to the Green River at a spectacular place called the Gates of Lodore. The name was coined by Major John Wesley

Powell during his epic journey down the Green and Colorado Rivers in 1869. He took the name from an English poem, "How the Waters Come Down at Lodore," which he would recite as he and his men drifted down the turbulent rivers.

Powell's journey began north of here at the town of Green River, Wyoming, in early May 1869. It was an amazing feat, charting the largely unknown land and waters of that vast, rugged, inhospitable tableland known as the Colorado Plateau. Not only did the group prove the navigability, albeit difficult in places, of the Green and Colorado Rivers, but they made important studies of the geology, flora, and fauna of the region as well. (Powell was a geology professor before he began his career as an explorer.) In late August, the men completed their journey below the great gorges

Piñon pine growing out of sandstone

of the Grand Canyon, where Lake Mead is located today. During the course of their trip, reports were widely circulated that the whole party had perished, but Powell eventually returned to Washington a hero. He obtained funds to repeat the trip in 1871 and later became the second director of the United States Geological Survey.

One of the most difficult parts of the journey began here, where the Green River enters a series of steep, narrow defiles at the Gates of Lodore. The group's greatest calamity occurred about ten miles downstream when they lost one of their boats, the "No Name," at a treacherous rapids they subsequently named Disaster Falls. Despite the perils, Powell found much to admire along this stretch of the river. In his now-famous journal, he wrote:

This has been a chapter of disasters and toils, notwithstanding which the Canyon of Lodore was not devoid of scenic interest, even beyond the power of pen to tell. The roar of its waters was heard unceasingly from the hour we entered it until we landed here [Echo Park, at the confluence with the Yampa River]. No quiet in all that time. But its walls and cliffs, its peaks

Yampa River emerging from Cross Mountain Gorge near Deerlodge Park in Dinosaur National Monument

and crags, its amphitheaters and alcoves, tell a story of beauty and grandeur that I hear yet—and shall hear.

Continuing north on Highway 318 past the turnoff for the Gates of Lodore, you enter Browns Park, a remote valley that was a favorite hangout of the mountain men in the 1830s and of Butch Cassidy and his Wild Bunch in the early 1890s. Today the valley is a national wildlife refuge, and you'll find it interesting just to wander around here. Both in the spring and fall, there are large numbers of waterfowl, including Canada geese, whistling swans, sandhill cranes, and several species of ducks. You're also likely to see small herds of pronghorn antelope.

Deerlodge Park

Compared to the other backroads tours of Colorado, the Deerlodge Park trip is short in distance traveled. But it has such appeal that you'll probably linger for a long while, especially if you make the trip under the same conditions I did.

It was early October when I turned off U.S. High-

Cottonwoods in autumn in Deerlodge Park

way 40 between Maybell and Elk Springs and followed the signs toward Deerlodge Park, in the southeastern corner of Dinosaur National Monument. The autumn color had long since disappeared from the High Country, but here the cottonwoods were a brilliant orange. It was also well past the peak of the tourist season, and even U.S. 40 had little traffic on it.

About five to six miles from the highway, after driving through gently rolling sage and piñon-covered hills, you'll catch your first sight of the Yampa River. The name is derived from the parsniplike plant whose root was a favorite food of the Native Americans. Each fall, several tribes migrated to the Yampa River Valley here in northwest Colorado to collect the nutty, sweet roots. The plant was also well known to early settlers, so much so in fact, that "Yampa" was a contender for the name of the state.

Pull into the marked scenic area where you first sight the river, for there is a breathtaking view of the gorge carved by the water. Here the Yampa emerges from between steep, sheer walls and meanders lazily through a broad valley for several miles before plunging into a series of great gorges to the west.

The road ends in another nine miles, just after entering Dinosaur National Monument. There is a small but lovely campground here, in a grove of huge cottonwood trees. This spot is so relaxing and inviting, you'll probably want to stay awhile. And that's what I did. I expected to see at least one or two other cars pull into the camping area before nightfall, but I had the place to myself. In fact, I never saw another soul that afternoon or the next day. As the sun dipped toward the sandstone rim beyond the campground, I cooked a small supper and enjoyed the play of twilight colors on the cottonwoods. My tranquil mood was somewhat disturbed, however, when two magpies flew into a nearby cottonwood and took up a silent vigil for food morsels.

Magpies are generally cautious birds, but these two seemed like old hands at campground larceny. As I sat there eating my canned stew and sipping wine from a tin cup, they glided down past the table for a closer look, landing on the ground only a few feet away from me. I tossed them a small piece of French bread and they pounced on it. After a brief squabble, one of the birds flew off with the tidbit. The other waddled indignantly over to me and demanded its share. I responded, and it too flew off with a small piece of bread.

I quickly realized that my generosity had been a mistake. In a few minutes, the panhandlers were back.

Even worse, they brought their whole gang with them, and soon there were almost a dozen magpies in the cottonwood, squawking loudly in threatening, demanding tones. I felt as though I had been thrust into the middle of a scene from Alfred Hitchcock's movie *The Birds.*

Trying to eat with dozens of greedy eyes watching was a bit uncomfortable, so I hastily finished my repast and went for a walk in the parklike grove of cottonwoods, swishing my feet through the litter of leaves. Three mule deer bounded up a sage-covered hillside, then stopped and stared at me while their ridiculous ears flopped incessantly to ward off a few bugs. It was nearly dark when I got back to the campground, and most of the magpies were gone. I threw a sleeping bag on the ground and slept out under a clear sky, riddled with stars.

Next morning, there was frost on the ground. I had a quick cup of tea, then went for another hike as the sun slanted through the trees and melted the frost. I made friends with several more mule deer before firing up the van for the drive back to U.S. 40. Didn't see anyone all the way back to the highway. A good spot to get away from it all.

The Valley of the White River

In 1868, the year he made his epic journey down the Green and Colorado Rivers, Major John Wesley Powell led an overland expedition down the valley of the White River. He later wrote, "the region is one of great desolation: arid, almost treeless, with bluffs, hills, ledges of rock and drifting sands."

Powell's description is perhaps better suited to that portion of the White River near its confluence with the Green, for the section from Meeker to Rangely along Colorado Highway 64 is quite beautiful. True, the surrounding hills are dry and desertlike, but the bottomlands are lush and fertile, with magnificent old cottonwoods scattered along the riverbanks.

I began the tour in Meeker a few miles west of the intersection of Colorado Highways 789 and 132. The town was named for Nathan C. Meeker, an inept but well-meaning Indian agent who in 1879, along with nine other employees of the White River Agency, was killed by his charges, the northern Utes, in a revolt his blunderings incited. The intervention of Chief Ouray, an articulate and intelligent leader of the southern Utes (see "Colorado Sketch: Chief Ouray"), prevented more bloodshed. About three miles west of here, just

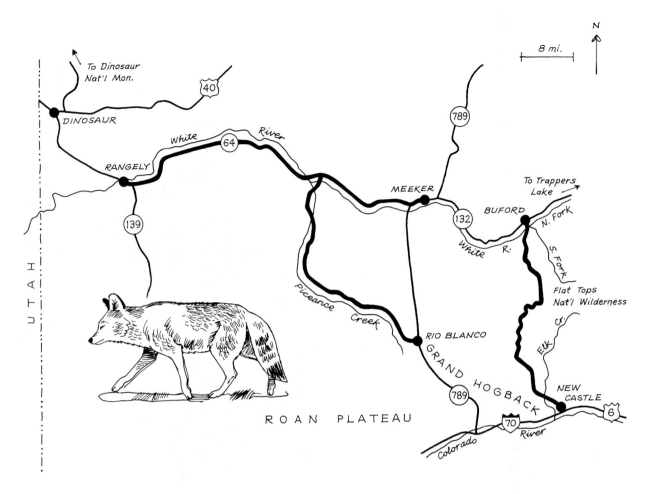

The White River Valley, New Castle, and Buford

off Highway 64, is a monument marking the spot where the fight, known today as the "Meeker Massacre," took place. (This is the same Meeker who in 1870 had founded the town of Greeley.)

About twenty miles west of Meeker, Highway 64 is intersected by an unmarked road; a drive along this backroad makes a worthwhile trip. Running south and east for thirty miles, the route parallels Piceance Creek. (*Piceance* is a Ute word meaning "tall grass.") The road winds through towering sandstone bluffs in the heart of the mountain-plateau-desert transition region of Colorado. Today the area is the center of an environmental controversy, for this is oil shale country and there is considerable concern over the potential harm to the land by strip mining. Fortunately, with cheaper and more ecologically sound energy alternatives emerging, full-scale development of these oil shales seems deferred, at least for now. The road ends at the town of Rio Blanco near the southwestern

corner of the Flat Tops. Turn left here on Highway 789 to return to Meeker.

If you choose not to take the Piceance Creek side trip, however, you can continue west on Highway 64 through more of the verdant White River Valley to Rangely.

New Castle to Buford

I turned off Interstate 70 at New Castle, an old mining camp named for the well-known English coal mining town, because I was curious about the backroad shown on my map that heads north to Buford through a part of the White River National Forest. This is the western edge of the Flat Tops country (described in "Part I: The High Country"), and I anticipated some great scenery. I wasn't disappointed.

A few miles north of New Castle, the paved road becomes graveled as it begins to climb gradually out

Above: *The valley of the White River*
Right: *Geese at play in front of an abandoned school along Highway 64 in the White River Valley*

Chief Ouray

Every once in a while, a great statesman comes along. Sometimes, if he's in the right spot at the right time, he can change history. Sometimes, history just flows right over him like an unchecked tidal wave, and such was the case with the Ute Chief Ouray.

Some say the fact that he was born in 1833, the year of one of the most fantastic meteorite displays in history, was an omen that he was destined for greatness. His upbringing certainly had a lot to do with his career as a statesman. Born of an Apache father and a Ute mother, he was reared in the household of a loving Spanish family near Taos, New Mexico. By the time he rejoined the Uncompahgre Utes as a teenager, he spoke several languages and was at home with three of the major cultures of the Southwest: Spanish, Anglo, and Ute. Unknowingly, he had been trained for statesmanship as carefully as any prince is trained for ruling a country.

Given this background, Ouray probably had more insight into what was going on in the West than the average person of his time. And what he observed happening to his people he didn't like. A trip through the newly discovered gold fields near Denver increased his concern. It would be only a matter of time, he felt, before the hordes of gold- and land-crazy white men would take over all the Native lands in Colorado.

It was clear to Ouray, who was by now chief of the Uncompahgre Utes, that his people needed a treaty outlining what lands were to be theirs. In 1863, such a treaty was signed. The Utes were granted all of the Colorado land west of the Continental Divide—"forever"—but they agreed to give up mineral rights to the territory in exchange for $20,000 worth of goods annually for ten years.

In five years, under pressure from Colorado mining interests, Washington was ready to write another treaty. Actually, so was Ouray. He had formulated a new plan for all the Colorado Utes and was chosen to be their spokesman at the treaty table.

First, he'd make sure they had a reservation of their own, land no white man could take away from

Chief Ouray and his wife, Chipeta (Photo courtesy the Library of Congress)

them. Then, he'd gradually wean the Utes from their strictly hunting economy and develop one that would allow them to survive in the modern world. Their new economy would include stock raising and increased trade with the whites. And with honest Indian agents on the reservation to assure that the annuities granted by the government would not consist of spoiled supplies, the Utes should be able to manage quite well.

If Washington thought Ouray would be a pushover at the treaty talks, they were dead wrong. The Indians came out on top. The treaty of 1868 gave them a reservation of sixteen million acres on the Western Slopes of Colorado, far more than the small southwestern corner of the state that the politicians wanted to cede them. The reservation would have two agencies: the White River Agency for the use of the northern Utes and the Los Pios Agency for the southern Utes. The Utes were also to get $50,000 worth of supplies every year. Furthermore and perhaps most important, white settlers and miners were specifically prohibited from passing through the Ute territory. Ouray had succeeded in attaining the first part of his economic goal.

Meanwhile, back in the gold fields, there were bigger and better strikes. When gold was discovered in the San Juan Mountains, miners flocked there by the hundreds. The fact that this was Ute land didn't bother them a bit, but it did bother the Utes. Obviously, something had to be done.

It was. In 1873, Ouray and representatives of all the other Ute nations met with a special Indian Bureau commission. The result was the Brunot Treaty, which ceded four million acres of the San Juan Mountains back to the whites for hunting privileges and $25,000 a year for the rest of time. The lust for gold had won.

Ouray knew that this treaty was the only way short of warfare—which would be genocidal—to keep the Utes from being pushed out of Colorado altogether. His biggest task now was to try to prevent any Ute hotbloods from precipitating an incident that would give the whites an excuse to rescind all the hard-fought treaties and move the Utes to some God-forsaken land outside of Colorado. It would not be easy.

While Ouray was admired and respected by both whites and Indians for his statesmanship, he had made some enemies in his rise to power. And as one chief among many, he had never been able to speak for all Indians any more than the governor of one state can speak for all Americans. The dissidents viewed the Brunot Treaty as evidence that Ouray and the other chiefs who had agreed to it had sold out to the whites. The northern Utes from the White River Agency especially gave Ouray nightmares.

Six years after the signing of the Brunot Treaty, everything Ouray had worked for collapsed. Given the anti-Indian temper of the times and the growing "Utes must go" sentiment, it's amazing it took that long for the precipitating incident to occur. But it's not surprising that when it did, it happened at the White River Agency.

Nathan C. Meeker, honest but idealistic to a fault, was appointed Indian agent of the northern Utes. He was absolutely determined that for their own good, his Utes would give up hunting for agriculture. The Utes were not particularly interested in becoming farmers, but they humored him until he did the unpardonable. He plowed up their pony racetrack and pony pasture. They were as furious as present-day Denverites would be if someone plowed up Mile High Stadium, home of the Denver Broncos.

As the tension between whites and Utes mounted, Meeker called for military protection. In response to the advance of the troops, the northern Utes burned the agency buildings; killed all the white men at the post, including Meeker; and took Meeker's daughter, wife, and another white woman and her two small children captive.

Ouray was heartsick. He sent a message to the northern Utes calling for the end of hostilities. His action and the arrival of more troops brought about an end to the fighting. Then he helped negotiate for the release of the captives, thinking perhaps if they were returned unharmed, it would help the Utes' cause.

A month later, the hostages were released but by then nothing could help the Utes, particularly after the women revealed that the Indians had taken certain "liberties" with them.

Still, Ouray tried. Although sick with nephritis, he went to Washington to try to get the best possible terms for his people in the renegotiation of territorial treaties and to keep a government investigating committee from being too harsh with the guilty Utes.

Then he accepted the thankless task of getting his people to sign the treaty that would move them to three new reservations. One of these was in Utah and the second on the New Mexico–Colorado border. The third reservation was to be located around the confluence of the Colorado (at that time called the Grand) and Gunnison Rivers near present-day Grand Junction, if suitable land could be found there.

Ouray died in August 1880. He was forty-eight. A year later, no suitable land having been found near Grand Junction, his people were herded to a new reservation in Utah. Only a band of southern Utes remained in Colorado, on a small strip of land in the southwest corner of the state, with a still smaller section extending into New Mexico.

Chief Ouray was not forgotten. In 1900, it was decided to choose sixteen people from the ranks of famous Colorado citizens of the past to comprise a state Hall of Fame. Their portraits, done in stained glass, would adorn the dome of the new Capitol. Chief Ouray was the second person chosen for the honor.

View west from the Buford–New Castle road in the White River National Forest

of the farming and ranching valley of Elk Creek. (How many Elk Creeks are there in the West, I wondered. In my travels in the Rockies, I'll bet I have seen, drunk from, crossed over, or fallen into more than a hundred of them. The same is true of Bear Creeks, Rattlesnake Creeks, and Deer Creeks.)

In about ten miles, I entered the northwestern unit of the White River National Forest. Established in 1891 to preserve the scenic resources around the headwaters of the White River, the National Forest experienced a devastating infestation of spruce bark beetles a few decades ago. In many places here, there are silvery, ghostlike remains of the dead trees still standing. Though severe at times, such infestations of tree-killing beetles are now understood by ecologists to play a role in long-term forest ecology by thinning extremely dense stands of trees and opening up areas for eventual replacement by other tree species. I saw some

stands of dead spruce on this trip but, for the most part, the forest seemed fully recovered and healthy.

After climbing steeply, the road levels out and for miles traverses rolling parklike country, the vast swales of grass interspersed with coniferous forest. In several places, there are beautiful views of the Roan Plateau and the ridge called Grand Hogback.

A number of side roads along this route lead to trail heads for trips into the Flat Tops National Wilderness. There are several U.S. Forest Service campgrounds here, and I stopped for lunch at one of them. Two gray white Canada jays, or "camp robbers," flew down from a nearby tree and insisted on sharing my peanut butter-and-jelly sandwich. These large and handsome birds are quite familiar in most Colorado campgrounds. They've become expert panhandlers; in fact, they are so brazen at times that they will literally eat out of your hand.

The upper White River Valley along the Buford–New Castle road

Heading north through the forest again, I came over a small rise and spotted something crossing the road in the distance. As I approached, it darted into the forest. When I got closer, I stopped. Then I saw a gray-brown form loping casually through the trees—a coyote. It halted for a moment to check me out, its ears standing sharply erect and pointed, its eyes fixed on me. Then it turned and disappeared into a draw. I left with a nice feeling, knowing that at least a few coyotes around here hadn't been hunted, poisoned, or trapped.

Eventually the road descends into the quiet and peaceful valley of the White River. In the town of Buford, it intersects Colorado Highway 132. Continuing to the right on an unmarked road, you can reach Trappers Lake and another part of the lovely Flat Tops country. I turned left and headed toward Meeker.

Grand Mesa

One of Western Colorado's most prominent landforms, Grand Mesa is indeed grand. This fifty-square-mile flat-topped plateau rises more than 5,000 feet above the bordering Gunnison and Colorado River valleys. With an elevation of between 10,000 and 11,000 feet above sea level, the mesa's climate and vegetation vary enormously from its base to its top. In the lowlands of the Gunnison and Colorado Rivers, the average annual precipitation is only about eight inches, whereas the cooler plateau top receives about thirty inches and lies deeply blanketed in snow much of the year. The result of these extremes in climate and weather is a remarkable series of vegetative zones in a relatively short distance. In climbing toward the summit of Grand Mesa by any one of four roads, you pass through four distinct biological regions: the Upper

Sonoran, Transitional, Montane, and Subalpine zones, representing the equivalent encountered in a journey of several thousand miles northward.

For anyone interested in geology, a trip to the top of the vast mesa provides a fascinating look at a record of sedimentary strata and the effects wrought by ancient volcanism and the forces of wind and water.

I began my own Grand Mesa trip northeast of Grand Junction where U.S. Highway 6 crosses the Colorado River just east of De Beque. Heading west, watch for an obscure road on the left with a sign pointing the way to Mesa. My reason for choosing this particular route (there are more direct approaches) was one of those symbols on my road map that indicate unusual features. In this case, it said, "Paintpot Country." Being a backroad freak, I was compelled to check it out. However, darkness began to close in on me soon after I turned off the main highway, so I pulled off the dirt road into a sandy draw and camped amid some fragrant piñon pines, junipers, and sagebrush.

The next morning, I continued on my trek, heading south, and soon discovered the origin of the name on the map. This is incredibly austere country of sandstone buttes eroded into creased hills, carved canyons, and stone towers, all in multicolored hues ranging from slate gray to white to buff to orange to deep maroon. As I neared the intersection of Colorado Highway 165, I also got my first glimpse of Grand Mesa. Rising abruptly above a sea of green forest, it was rimmed along its flat top by snow.

The next portion of the trip took me through the lovely hamlet of Mesa on Highway 65. Soon the road begins to climb in gradual, sweeping curves up the plateau's northern edge, and during the ascent, there's another of those transitions in season. The valley around Mesa was hot and summery when I was there in late May. As the road gained in altitude, the deep green foliage of the aspen was replaced by a lighter, fresher verdancy, then brown buds, then totally bare branches near the mesa top. As I drove along the flat summit through dark coniferous forests, snow lay deep in shady places, and some of the lakes were rimmed with ice. Farther south toward the interior of the mesa, the snow became deeper alongside the road, lakes were frozen, and a brisk, cold wind let you know that it was still winter here.

South of Skyway (a resort and a few stores), I turned right, taking the marked turnoff to Lands End, intrigued by the name. The dirt road winds through meadows and sparse forests, touched here and there

with the incipient green of spring. Apparently this area closest to the mesa's western edge has a more moderate climate than the interior because of the warm westerly winds raised from the mild valley below. But as I was about to discover, the wind on this particular day was far from warm.

Approaching the rim of the mesa near Shirttail Point, I spotted an unusual phenomenon: trees and rocks coated thickly with ice. The source, I found, was a waterfall that plunged over the mesa's lip and was whipped into spray by cold winds. I got out to photograph the scene, only to discover that the winds were no gentle zephyrs funneling up from the valley below. I literally had to hold the camera and tripod down in order to take a picture, and in the time it took to accomplish this task, I nearly suffered frostbite! I later estimated the air temperature to be a few degrees above freezing, but the wind velocity of well over fifty miles per hour (a conservative estimate) made the wind-chill factor about zero.

At Lands End, the road descends five thousand feet in a series of spectacular switchbacks. The views of the Gunnison Valley and the distant Grand Valley around Grand Junction are superb. And when I arrived at U.S. Highway 50, in the valley once more, the temperature was nearly eighty degrees. This trip ranks among the most beautiful, exciting, and varied of my backroads tours of Colorado.

Vancorum to Grand Junction

The terrain through which you drive on this trip, from Vancorum to Uravan to Gateway to Grand Junction by way of Colorado Highway 141 and U.S. Highway 50, bears a striking resemblance to that of Monument Valley and certain other parts of northern Arizona. It seems impossible that the weirdly carved landscape could be part of Colorado—impossible, that is, if you visualize the state's scenery as consisting solely of forested slopes, snowcapped mountains, and prairie.

You can begin the trip at Grand Junction or, as I did, at Naturita, on Colorado Highways 141 and 90. Vancorum is about two miles northwest of here, and just beyond the town, Highway 141 becomes a scenic route. The road parallels the San Miguel River for about ten miles, then runs along the Dolores after the two rivers merge north of Uravan.

Uravan is named for the uranium and vanadium mined and refined in the region, but the town of Uravan doesn't officially exist anymore. And the zip code of this former town of one thousand residents

The road up Grand Mesa in springtime

has been reassigned. Uravan died because of a declining market for its primary industrial product, uranium. Unfortunately, the byproduct of this industry—radioactive mine tailings—is still here and in the process of being removed to a burial site above Uravan.

Over eons of time, the rushing waters of the Dolores River have cut a steep gorge in the brilliant red and orange sandstone. Following the course of the rivers, you'll have superb views of the canyon and the surrounding countryside.

A few miles north of Uravan is a turnoff and overlook. Here you can see the remnants of an old wooden flume on the sheer walls of the canyon below. Built in the early 1890s, the six-mile-long wooden channel was intended to carry water to some arid, gold-bearing placer deposits downstream. Workmen were lowered in cradles from the canyon rim to affix the wooden trough to the vertical walls of the cliff. Although $173,000 were spent on the project, it was abandoned after a few years because the deposits yielded little gold. Today parts of the old flume cling precariously to the canyon walls as a monument to gold-crazed perseverance.

Between Uravan and Gateway, the canyon alter-

Above: *The seasonal progression of foliage on Grand Mesa: aspen leafing out on the lower ridge and those still waiting to bud on the upper ridge*
Left: *Frost-covered trees on the top of Grand Mesa in springtime*

Escalante and Domínguez

As the literature published during the U.S. Bicentennial occasionally pointed out, there were other events besides the signing of the Declaration of Independence that took place in July 1776. While those earnest colonists in Philadelphia were drafting the document that would end British domination in the East, a band of equally earnest men in Santa Fe, New Mexico, was preparing an expedition designed to ensure Spanish domination in the West.

The Spanish were the earliest white settlers in the Southwest, but just being first didn't mean much. You had to hold on once you were there. And the Spanish remembered that their missionaries and soldiers had been pushed out of the area, if only temporarily, by an uprising of the Pueblo. Now, the Spanish authorities in the New World were getting increasingly nervous about the English, French, and Russian explorations of the far West. Finding a route that would connect the remote settlements in New Mexico to the missions in California for the purposes of communication and defense was considered to be of the utmost importance.

The men chosen for the job were two Franciscan friars, Fray Silvestre Vélez de Escalante and Fray Francisco Atanasio Domínguez. Escalante had had a little experience in the exploring business—thirteen days the previous year spent visiting the Moqui (Hopi) pueblos and trying to get to the Grand Canyon of the Colorado.

Escalante and Domínguez led their band of eight men out of Santa Fe on July 29, 1776. When they reached a place near the site of present-day Pagosa Junction, they had crossed into territory that exactly one hundred years later would become Colorado. From there the route they followed would take them through some of the roughest and some of the most beautiful terrain in Colorado.

The first part of their course had been explored before, by Juan Maria Rivera in 1765. One of Rivera's men was now with the Escalante group as an official guide. He led them to the Dolores River and its steep-sided canyon. They had a little trouble getting across it: They seemed always to be either too high above the water or too confined in the bottom of the canyon.

By the time the group reached the even more difficult, barren canyon country around the present-day town of Bedrock, they figured they'd better give up on the "official" guide and find an Indian one. Heading east, they entered the Uncompahgre Valley and then followed the North Fork of the Gunnison. At this point, they finally found a guide. It took a bit of persuasion; the other Indians thought they were crazy to continue.

The party traveled over the top of Grand Mesa, went down its northern side, and came to the Colorado River near what is now De Beque. Here the Colorado is just another river and easy to cross.

Heading northwest through the Roan Plateau to the White River at present-day Rangely and then west, they entered Utah. Continuing west to Utah Lake, the group turned south to Sevier Lake and finally came to the Virgin River in the southwestern corner of Utah.

By now it was winter, complete with snow. Discretion won over valor, and Escalante and Domínguez decided to turn back to Santa Fe. But rather than trying to retrace their circuitous route, they attempted a shortcut straight east.

This meant they would have to recross the Colorado River, which would prove to be a truly terrifying experience. That innocent little river they had crossed in Colorado was a torrent at the bottom of the Grand and Glen Canyons in Arizona and Utah.

They tried to ford the river at what is now Lees Ferry, Arizona, just south of the Utah border, but couldn't make it. Climbing back up to the rim, they traveled along the north rise of Glen Canyon and finally, at a point that would ever after be known as "The Crossing of the Fathers," found a place where they could swim across.

They had no idea how lucky they were to have found that spot. Major John Wesley Powell, after his famous trip down the Colorado River ninety years later, said he knew of only two places in five hundred miles where the river could be reached from the rim—Lees Ferry and The Crossing of the Fathers.

After this ordeal, the rest of the trip to Santa Fe must have seemed easy. The party arrived home on January 2, 1777. From this point on, the careers of the two friars became obscure, and they disappeared from history. We're not even sure when they died.

Escalante and Domínguez had not found a

route from Santa Fe to California, so their superiors undoubtedly considered them colossal failures. But were they?

They had traveled two thousand miles over extremely difficult terrain in five months, exploring a huge inland region that had theretofore been virtually ignored. And the route they followed did eventually serve as the basis for part of the Old Spanish Trail, which went from Santa Fe to California.

Escalante had kept a meticulous journal during the expedition. In the days when many explorers looked upon a rugged landscape as something to be endured and conquered, Escalante saw beauty in it. His descriptions reveal his great appreciation of the magnificent rivers, mountains, and forests in the areas through which his party traveled. His reports of the journey are valued by historians. The world should have more of these "failures."

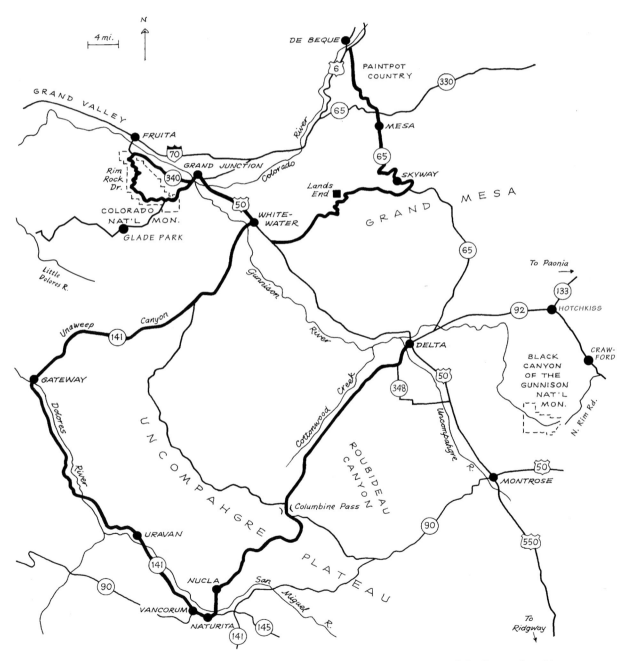

Grand Mesa, Vancorum, Grand Junction, Colorado National Monument, the Dolores River, and the Uncompahgre Plateau

nates between a steep, narrow gorge and a broad, open valley where the Dolores meanders placidly. The brown, sediment-laden waters of the river are fringed by feathery, lavender-blossomed tamarisks and by cool, green cottonwood trees. It is in this section that the scenery becomes so reminiscent of northern Arizona. Great sandstone buttes and mesas rise hundreds of feet above the valley. Erosion has created numerous towers and stone goblins in a variety of shapes. Side canyons invite a short hike to see what mysteries lie beyond the first bend. (Some ancient cliff dwellings? Cool, shaded alcoves? Perhaps a deep, cold spring beneath a towering wall?) Incipient arches in the form of conchoidal depressions lie at the bases of smooth, orange walls. Along the highway and the river's edge wave blossoms of scarlet gilia, orange globe mallow, and yellow princess plume. The area is a perfect example, in all its geological and biological forms, of the great slickrock country of the vast Colorado Plateau country.

At Gateway, the highway heads northeast, leaving the Dolores River, which plunges on into a series of canyons before joining the Colorado River. This section of the road passes through Unaweep Canyon, which is also colorful sandstone country, then the landscape makes a subtle transition as you climb gradually up the northern edge of the Uncompahgre Plateau. Green, cultivated fields of farms and ranches contrast with the brilliant rocks. But soon the red sandstone is replaced by more austere brown and gray tones. Finally, white and buff sandstone walls line the road as you descend the last few miles to U.S. 50 at Whitewater, southeast of Grand Junction in the broad, arid valley of the Gunnison River.

From Whitewater, it's a short distance to Grand Junction, where you have the opportunity to take an interesting side trip to Colorado National Monument, a twenty-eight-square-mile area of grotesquely carved and fantastically colored sandstone canyons and monoliths. You really shouldn't pass this up.

At Grand Junction, turn off onto Colorado Highway 340 for the ten-mile drive that leads directly to the monument's northern entrance. There's a campground close by if you want to relax a bit before continuing, because an exciting twenty-two-mile automobile ride along Rim Rock Drive lies ahead of you. Parking overlooks are located to provide views of the most unusual sandstone formations. The highlight of the drive on this road is the steep, serpentine ascent (known as the Trail of the Serpent) up to aptly named Cold Shivers Point on the brink of a precipice one

San Miguel River near Vancorum in the Uncompahgre Plateau region

thousand feet high. Rim Rock Drive runs into Highway 340, which takes you back to Grand Junction.

Colorado National Monument to the Dolores River

Colorado National Monument has become a popular place for tourists, particularly since it's just a short side trip from well-traveled Interstate 70. Preserved in the monument are monolithic sandstone formations typical of those found throughout the vast Colorado Plateau comprising western Colorado and much of Utah and northern Arizona. This plateau is a network of intricately carved canyons and gorges, large and small, created by the Colorado River and its numerous tributaries. In fact, here at Colorado National Monument you are rarely out of sight of the Colorado River flowing past in the broad valley to the north. The monument is a worthwhile visit, giving a flavor of some of the spectacular sandstone country of Utah.

There is a side trip that begins in Colorado National Monument, one that isn't as spectacular as the monument itself but gives a glimpse of some pleasant, rarely visited country. If you enter the monument from the Grand Junction entrance, the road climbs steeply in a series of switchbacks, passes through a

Grand Junction sandstone monoliths in Ute Canyon in the Colorado National Monument

tunnel carved in the sandstone, then levels out at Cold Shivers Point. Just beyond the Cold Shivers viewpoint take the road to the left; the sign points the way to Glade Park. This road skirts the boundary of the monument and the edge of No Thoroughfare Canyon (again, another apt name as you'll see from its ruggedness). Incidentally, there is another road that will take you to Glade Park and is closer if you enter the monument from the West or Fruita Entrance. Follow the Rim Rock Drive past the park headquarters and visitor center. About two miles past Artist Point, a road takes off to the right (marked with a sign pointing to Glade Park).

Glade Park is a crossroads with a delightful, even classic, general store. There's also a restaurant. If you have half a tank or less of gas, you should fill up here—there is no gas ahead. Might also be a good idea to fill up the cooler with ice and some cold drinks. You're heading into desert country.

West of Glade Park the road descends gradually toward the drainage of the Dolores River. Ahead in the shimmering heat waves are mesas and canyons of eastern Utah. As you head west, you'll notice a gradual change in the vegetation to a drier, desert ecosystem. Predominate plants here are the piñon pine, junipers, and yucca. If you make this trip in May or June, particularly if there have been some spring rains, the desert wildflowers will be a riot of color: scarlet globemallow, red and yellow pricklypear cactus, creamy yucca blossoms, pink and red skyrocket gilia, and others. One of my favorites, and not common, is the claret cup cactus whose blossoms are a deep, vivid red.

As enhancement to the feeling that you've entered desert country there are some lovely sand dunes a few miles before you reach the Little Dolores River. The sand is fine and orange in color. From here you have a superb view of the snowcapped La Sal Mountains in Utah.

Depending on the time of year you visit here, there may or may not be water in the Little Dolores River. If there has been a lot of snow in the High Country, or if there have been heavy rains, the river may be impassable at times in May or June. Other times it is dry or nearly so, and you can traverse it. However, from this point on, the road gets quite rough in places and if you plan to get to the Dolores River itself, four-wheel drive is definitely recommended.

Actually, the Little Dolores is a good destination by itself. The small stream is lined with big cottonwoods, offering shady spots for a picnic lunch. One

year here there was enough water in June to splash around in and submerge ourselves in some small pools shared with numerous tadpoles. A thoroughly delightful place.

Because this trip can take the better part of a day, you may want to camp. Another option is to backtrack to the Glade Park Store and stay overnight in one of the two suites they have available. (Make a reservation first, on your way through Glade Park.) This second option will allow you to get an early start to explore another area, Rattlesnake Canyon.

If you head north from Glade Park toward Colorado National Monument, watch for the signs on the left pointing the way to Rattlesnake Canyon. This side road is about eight to ten miles long and your vehicle should have good ground clearance. At its end is a trailhead leading into a fascinating area of sandstone canyons and wind-carved arches. This is the largest concentration of sandstone arches outside of Utah. Although the hike is only about five miles round-trip, allow plenty of time to enjoy the beauty of the area. And be sure to carry sufficient water with you, especially if you visit in the hot summer months. An early start is advisable to avoid the terrific heat of midday.

Uncompahgre Plateau

In a sense, the Uncompahgre Plateau might be termed a Grand Mesa that didn't quite make it. Or perhaps it's still in the making. Raised above the surrounding region by gradual uplifting, the plateau is nearly as high and as flat as Grand Mesa. However, erosion forces over eons of time have smoothed the edges of the tableland so that its contours are less jagged and, from most approaches, less spectacular than those of its counterpart forty miles away, across the Gunnison Valley. But this area has a beauty and grandeur of its own. (If you are wondering about the odd name, it is derived from a Ute word meaning "red water canyon" or, according to other interpretations, "stinking waters.")

In the town of Delta near the convergence of the Gunnison and Uncompahgre Rivers take Colorado Highway 348. (The signs here point the way to Nucla.) About six miles southwest of the town, the highway turns sharply left, but you should continue straight ahead on the unmarked road and follow the Uncompahgre National Forest access signs. In these first few miles of the trip, you might spot evidence of an unusual problem for this agricultural area (Delta is in the center of the state's largest fruit-growing re-

Above: *Uncompahgre River in the Montrose region, with Owl Creek Pass in the distance*
Overleaf: *Highway 141 to Gateway on the Uncompahgre Plateau*

gion). Underlying a large part of the valley and of the Grand Valley to the north are deposits of salt-laden Mancos shale. Gradually, leeching of the salt and its deposition on bottomlands result not only in soil with a high alkalinity but also in such a concentration of salt that the deposits can actually be seen as white encrustations on some of the farmland. Scientists are currently working on methods of halting and reversing this salt buildup, which ultimately destroys the land's productivity.

The road soon climbs above the farmlands and enters a zone of extreme aridity. So sparse is vegetation that the land here resembles a moonscape in places. But almost immediately, some of the region's most striking features come into view. On the left is Roubideau Canyon, an eroded and colorful sandstone gorge resembling a scaled-down Grand Canyon. A stream winds through the canyon bottom, and lush grasses and cottonwoods contrast with the surrounding barren land. (An inviting place for some future exploration, I noted.) On the right, the land drops away steeply into Cottonwood Canyon, not quite as deep as Roubideau but equally colorful.

Gradually, more vegetation appears alongside the road: piñon pine and juniper, then scrub oak. Finally you enter the fringes of coniferous forests mixed with

143

stands of aspen. For miles, the majestic white-barked trees line the road, and here and there you pass an old ranch with rail fences of aspen stacked in a zigzag pattern.

At Columbine Pass (elevation 8,500 feet), the road divides. Turn left—the road to the right leads to Unaweep Canyon and to the northernmost edge of the Uncompahgre Plateau—and, in a mile or so, turn right following the signs to Nucla. (Taking the second road left when you leave Columbine Pass will lead you to a juncture with Colorado Highway 90 and northeast to Montrose.)

As the road to Nucla begins its descent of the southwestern edge of this vast mesa, there are superb views of Lone Cone Peak far to the south. Lone Cone is a 12,613-foot snowcapped pyramid jutting skyward over the land like a lonely sentinel.

Right away, you'll note a difference between the western and eastern flanks of the Uncompahgre Plateau. The western side apparently receives much more moisture, for the land is far less austere and there is a considerable variety of vegetation all the way to the valley floor near Nucla. It seems likely that, because of its great size and relative height, the Uncompahgre Plateau influences weather patterns of the region. Air masses blown in by prevailing westerly winds are raised and chilled, causing them to release moisture as rain and snow. This "wringing" effect in the west leaves the eastern and northern parts of the plateau more arid.

Crossing some streams dammed by beavers, the

Above: *Cattle drive blocking the road near Nucla on the Uncompahgre Plateau*
Left: *Road to Nucla on the west side of the Uncompahgre Plateau*

Above: *Black Canyon of the Gunnison River from North Rim in the Black Canyon National Monument*
Right: *Courthouse Mountain viewed from the road near the summit of Owl Creek Pass*

road dips into a valley, then ascends a rise before dropping down into the lush farmlands of the San Miguel Valley, where it intersects Colorado Highway 141.

Owl Creek Pass

It was spring—early May as I remember—when I set out to explore the Owl Creek Pass region east of the Uncompahgre Valley. I had been on the road for several days on a photo assignment, documenting environmental problems in certain parts of Colorado, and frankly, I was tired of photographing junkyards, litter, and pollution. Time to capture some of Colorado's beauty as well, I thought. So as I was tooling south on U.S. Highway 550 on my way toward Ouray, I got hooked by that old backroad syndrome when I spotted a dirt road leading left and a sign that said, "Owl Creek Pass." The road begins where Colorado Highway 62 ends close to Ridgway. My map showed that it ascended the pass, then descended to the Cimarron River and followed it north to U.S. Highway 50 near Black Canyon of the Gunnison National Monument, where the Gunnison River has carved a spectacular sheer-walled canyon. Should be an interesting trip, I thought.

The weather was pleasant—hot, in fact—when I turned left just east of Ridgway and followed the dusty road in its gradual climb. The views southwest across the Uncompahgre Valley toward snow-covered Mount Sneffels (14,150 feet in elevation) and other peaks of the San Juan Mountains were spectacular. Ahead were the rugged pinnacles of Courthouse Mountain.

Springtime in the Rockies is, indeed, something special. Take an ample quantity of solar energy, add a liberal dash of melting snow, top it off with a profusion of wildflowers, and you have some of the ingredients of its splendor.

Within a few miles of the main highway, I began to realize that I was passing through a transition in seasons. The valley, as I said, was hot. It was early summer here—green meadows, cottonwoods in full leaf. As the road ascended, the scrub oaks were not only leafed out but beginning to look somewhat dry and dusty. Farther on, the quaking aspen were a deep green, the leaves fluttering in the slightest breeze. Soon I reached an elevation where the groves of aspen were

Cottonwood Pass on the Uncompahgre Plateau

150

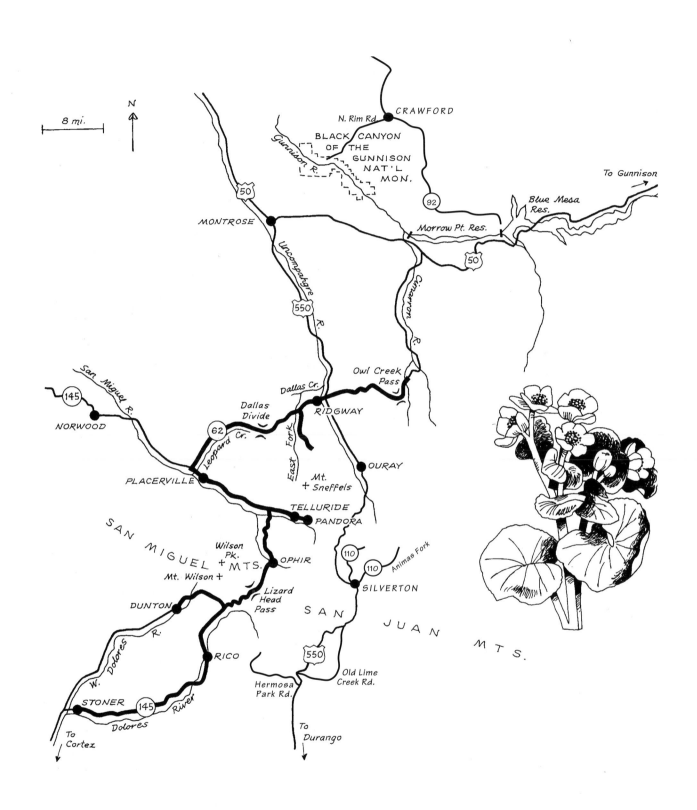

Owl Creek Pass, the Animas River, Hermosa Park Road, Old Lime Creek Road, Ridgway, San Miguel Valley,
Lizard Head Pass, the Dolores River, and Dunton

Water wagon in Silverton circa 1887 (Photo courtesy of Library, The State Historical Society of Colorado)

just beginning to be touched with a blush of spring green, a color that almost rivals the autumn gold in brilliance.

Continuing on, I moved into an earlier and earlier spring landscape and soon the incipient aspen leaves were tucked tightly into their pointed buds. There was evidence that the snow had been gone here only a short time: The grass was still dull brown and matted down. I did find one meadow with a southern exposure that was green and filled with thousands of marsh marigolds, so I stopped here to relax and have lunch.

As the road continued its upward climb and turned through dark, thick forests of Engelmann spruce and Douglas fir, I began to notices patches of snow. Soon the road grew wet and muddy and the snow patches coalesced into a continuous white in the forest and along the road's edge. Very early spring. But I knew, of course, that once I started down the other side of the pass into the Cimarron River Valley, I would soon be back to early summer.

Rounding a muddy curve, I found a thick patch

of snow several yards long in my path, so I gunned the van and zipped across it, the back wheels spinning and sliding. I figured that I must be near the top of the pass, and I hoped that I'd soon begin descending into warmer climes.

Wrong. I wheeled around one last muddy bend and my excursion was over. Ahead the road disappeared beneath an unbroken blanket of snow several feet thick. Winter.

I got out and explored on foot for a few hours, then retraced my path to camp for the night near the meadow full of marigolds. Next day I headed back down into the Uncompahgre Valley. Nothing wrong with seeing the same scenery twice when it's nice, but I made a promise to myself that I'd return to Owl Creek Pass sometime to see what the other side looks like. Soon I was back in summer again.

Later in the year I did return and made it to the other side. There's a lovely, short drive that takes you around the back side of Courthouse Mountain to an area of forests and meadows and a clear, rushing stream. And the road down the other side of Owl

Miners searching for gold placer particles circa 1880 (Photo courtesy of Library, The State Historical Society of Colorado)

Creek Pass is a pleasant drive that eventually joins U.S. Highway 50 near Cimarron.

The Animas River: Don't Drink the Water

U.S. Highway 550 south from Ridgway hardly qualifies as a backroad. But it is one of the more spectacular highways in the state, passing through the town of Ouray, then climbing in broad curves up to the 11,000-foot summit of Red Mountain Pass. It descends, amid equally spectacular scenery, to the town of Silverton. Silverton is noted as the terminus (or start, depending on your point of view) for the famed Durango-Silverton narrow-gauge railway. The train ride takes you through the canyon of the Animas River in the western part of the San Juan Mountains. Considered one the world's most scenic rail trips, it's a must for all railroad buffs. And since there is no road paralleling the railroad, it's the only way to this spectacular region.

Though I've extensively explored parts of western Colorado, for one reason or another I had never spent much time in the area of Silverton. And so, on a recent trip, I looked forward to exploring some of the area, particularly parts of the upper Animas River. I headed east of Silverton on Highway 110, paved for the first few miles, and then turning to gravel. I passed a mill of some sort, apparently a reclamation project, though not the kind that reclaims spoiled lands. Quite the opposite, in fact. The business here is reclaiming gold from old mine tailings. It's done by means of leaching ponds in which the old tailings are steeped in cyanide to dissolve the gold. These ponds are lined with plastic, which prevents the cyanide from leaking out into nearby streams and groundwater. Theoretically.

For several miles the road follows the upper Animas River or the Animas Fork. But what's left of the river and adjacent lands looks like a scene out of some horror/science fiction film—complete and utter devastation. This is an ecological disaster of the first magnitude. Hardly any plants grow in the broad valley of the river. And the river itself has been so disturbed by mining activity that it spreads itself in a few channels across a broad expanse of sterile rocks and gravel. Dead trees and stumps, bits of metal, and old tires decorate this moonscape. I continued on to the point where the road crosses the "river," then decided to turn around and get out of here. Except for views of rugged mountains in the distance, this undoubtedly qualifies as the ugliest backroad in Colorado.

Giving it one more try when I reached Silverton, I took another branch of Highway 110, this one climbing along forested mountainsides to the north of town. This route showed more promise. In a few miles, however, I discovered that this area, too, had been severely affected by mining.

The stream, a sizable flow of water and another tributary of the Animas River, was stained orange by some form of pollutant. I soon located the source (actually several sources)—old mines in the area whose tunnels and tailings piles were pouring out groundwater that had leached out minerals of various kinds. The main stream, in addition to the awful color of the rocks bordering it, had numerous stretches of green slime. The waters appeared lifeless, and that no one was fishing in this Colorado stream reinforced the fact that these poisons had killed off most everything. The road ended at another mine—actually another of those "reclamation" projects with evil-looking cyanide ponds. I backtracked in a hurry, anxious to leave this terribly scarred region.

Normally I would not have put this section in the book, preferring to write about those pleasant experiences in Colorado. But I feel compelled to point out that mining, often a romanticized part of Colorado's history, has had a devastating impact on some of Colorado's beauty and purity. If you are ever in the region of Silverton, you should see this for yourself. Just don't drink the water!

Hermosa Park Road

Hermosa Park is a beautiful little valley rimmed by thick forests of spruce. (The name is derived from the Spanish word for "beautiful.") This isn't a long trip, but one that's pleasant enough to make you want to linger. There are numerous places along the road where you can pull off and have a picnic. The stream here also invites wetting a fishing line.

You can begin this trip by pulling into the Purgatory Village, part of the Purgatory ski area on Highway 550 about twenty-five miles north of Durango. After entering the Village, watch for Forest Service signs to the right of the upper parking lot and follow the Hermosa Creek Road. In a mile or so the road forks; take the left fork, marked Forest Service Road 578. The fork that goes straight ahead is a worthwhile short jaunt known as the Cascade Divide Road. It climbs steeply and, in places, gives superb views of the main part of the San Juan Range to the east. It's worthwhile checking out, although watch out for logging trucks coming out of Relay Creek Road.

The Hermosa Park Road has a bit of interesting history behind it. It used to be part of the Pinkerton Trail and Scotch Creek Toll Road. Back in the 1870s, the town of Rico (on the other side of those mountains straight ahead as you travel down Hermosa Park) was booming; gold and silver were both being mined there. The big problem was transportation; Rico was far from the nearest railroad, and roads there were pretty out of the way. In the late 1870s, the Pinkerton Trail provided access from the rail line in the Animas Valley, east of here, over the mountains to Rico by way of Scotch Creek.

In 1882, the route was improved and changed, becoming known as the Scotch Creek Toll Road. But even this "improved" road was rough and rugged on man and beast. One commercial hauler, delivering two steam boilers, reported that he took thirty-five days with twenty-two yoke of oxen to make it from Rockwood (north of Durango) to Rico—a distance of thirty-five miles! In 1881, the Rio Grande Southern Railroad reached Rico, and the Scotch Creek Toll Road fell into disuse. Several miles down the Hermosa Park Road you can turn left and cross a stream (impassable in high water) to follow part of the old Scotch Creek Road, although most of it is considered to be for four-wheel drives only.

Following the main road down the valley takes you to a point where it crosses Hermosa Creek. If you have four-wheel drive, you can continue on up toward and over Bolsam Pass. We turned around here, backtracking into the main valley where we were greeted by one of those explosive Rocky Mountain thunderstorms. Rain poured down in blinding sheets and lightning crashed all around us. We pulled off the road to wait it out, cracking a hot thermos of coffee as we watched the drenching rain.

It was over in a half hour. I opened the car window to get some fresh air, and immediately we were overwhelmed by the fragrance of spruce trees. We headed back to a spot we had seen earlier, about halfway along the length of the valley, and pulled off to explore. It's a small, rocky bluff, flat on top and dropping off abruptly to the valley below. It has a pleasant

Aspen and spruce along the Hermosa Park Road in the Durango region

Aspen forest destroyed by winter avalanche along Old Lime Creek Road in the Silverton-Ouray region

Blue spruce seed cones along Hermosa Park Road

view across the valley to spruce-covered hillsides. The air was still perfumed by these conifers.

There are two types of spruce found here and in most parts of the state: the Colorado blue spruce (the state tree, naturally) and the Englemann spruce. Often I have difficulty telling apart the younger members of the two species. Blue spruce normally has needles of light silvery cerulean blue, but this isn't always the case. When growing in wet areas the needles can be green or yellow-green in color. Mature specimens of Englemann spruce are quite distinctive, with a scaly, reddish brown bark where the older blue spruce trees have a gray, furrowed bark. Either one is

a beautiful tree and lend a marvelous color (and odor) to this and other mountain regions of Colorado.

Old Lime Creek Road

Heading south from Silverton on Highway 550, the road climbs steeply out of the Animas River Valley and tops out at 10,910 feet in elevation at Molas Pass. A mile or so down the other side of the pass is a road that takes off to the left. "Old Lime Creek Road," according to the Forest Service sign. I'd passed by it on several occasions, but had never taken the time to check it out. On the map it seemed to be a short loop, rejoining the highway several miles below. Probably not very interesting, I thought. Boy, was I wrong.

Barbara and I had been staying at Purgatory for a few days, exploring the region, and while heading back down from Molas Pass one day, she said, "We ought to check out that road." Sure, why not. So I wheeled off the pavement and started down the steep incline of Old Lime Creek Road.

For the first couple of miles the road winds downward through aspen forests. We stopped to explore a small stream on the right, a series of small cascades in a narrow little gorge. A water ouzel, or dipper, was flitting from rock to rock, occasionally diving under water and emerging perfectly dry. These slate-gray birds feed on insect larvae and small fish. They build their nests perilously close to the water's edge, sometimes behind waterfalls. Perhaps their most distinguishing characteristic, however, is their habit of perching on a streamside rock and bobbing up and down with such vigor that they seem to be trying to launch themselves into space without benefit of wings.

The point where the road reaches its lowest elevation is alongside Lime Creek. It's a beautiful stream and there's a great campground here, although it appears to be little used. We lingered for a while, had lunch, walked leisurely through the forest.

Continuing on, we discovered one of those truly spectacular roads, a real white-knuckler. Leaving Lime Creek, the road climbs steeply and soon traverses a steep mountainside. Here, the track is literally blasted out of sheer rock. It's a long way down into that gorge below, but the views are terrific. Across the canyon we viewed some evidence of powerful natural forces at work. At the base of a steep avalanche chute, a large section of aspen forest had been flattened—apparently not long ago—by a big avalanche.

This section of road requires that you travel slowly. In places you can't see far enough ahead to determine if a vehicle is coming the other way. And the road is only wide enough for a single vehicle, with but a few spots where two cars might pass. This is definitely not Winnebago country. Fortunately there were no other cars, and eventually the road swings away from this steep canyon to meander gently through a forest of giant aspens before joining Highway 550 once again.

Ridgway to the San Miguel Valley

This tour, which begins in Ridgway, is not a long one in distance covered, but it can occupy a day or two because it takes you down along the East Fork of the Dallas Creek, where you'll want to linger before doubling back to the main road.

About twenty-five miles south of Montrose, U.S. Highway 550 runs into Colorado Highway 62, which heads west toward Dallas Divide. Less than a mile from the intersection is the town of Ridgway with many lovely old buildings dating from the area's boom days. At one time the town had been threatened by inundation from the waters of the Dallas Divide water project, but the reservoir was downsized and the town was spared.

Six miles southwest of Ridgway, turn left off Highway 62 and follow the U.S. Forest Service signs to the Dallas Creek East Fork campground. As you're driving the several miles to the campground, you have a continual view of the ragged spires of Mount Sneffels towering above the aspen and pines that line the road. The campground isn't particularly large, but when I got there I had it to myself and spent the afternoon exploring on foot the meadows and aspen groves nearby.

Perhaps the most striking feature of this area, aside from Mount Sneffels looming overhead, is the creek itself. In fact, it's one of the most beautiful mountain streams I've ever come across. I spent hours hiking alongside it and photographing its numerous cascades. The creek winds and tumbles through a thick forest of Engelmann and blue spruce, adding to the charm of this place. In the summer, delicate blossoms of red columbine wave along the rocky banks of the stream.

From the campground, there are trails that lead into the alpine country of the Mount Sneffels area. This range—and it is actually that rather than a single peak—has been preserved as the Mount Sneffels Wilderness Area. When you follow the road beyond the campground, you pass hillsides scarred from logging.

As the road continues, it twists and turns, gradually climbing, eventually becoming two dusty wheel ruts crossing a series of cattle guards. I pulled into an aspen grove and spent the afternoon lying in the hot sun in a marvelous meadow of wildflowers, eating a leisurely lunch and sipping wine while watching the clouds slip past the rugged peaks and planning some future hiking trips up into the mountains, and later, enjoying the play of sunset colors on the snowy top of Mount Sneffels. As I said, you'll want to linger.

When you return to Highway 62, turn left. As you continue west, the road climbs to the summit of Dallas Divide (elevation 8,970 feet). It is my personal

Mount Sneffels and the Sneffels Range near Dallas Divide

opinion that the views along this stretch of Highway 62 are some of the finest in Colorado, especially in autumn. In the foreground are spruce and aspen forests, lovely ranches and winding dirt roads lined with picturesque rail fences. To the south, of course, is the jagged outline of Mount Sneffels.

From Dallas Divide, the road drops steeply, cutting down through the colorful canyon carved by Leopard Creek, a tributary of the San Miguel River,

then comes to an end at Placerville, where it meets Colorado Highway 145.

Lizard Head Pass and the Dolores River

At Placerville—presumably named for the placer deposits of gold once found in the region—take Colorado Highway 145 to the left (south). If you turn right (north), this road winds through steep sandstone can-

Mount Wilson in the San Miguel Mountains near Telluride

yons of maroon-colored rock and leads to the little towns of Norwood, Redvale, and Naturita in the lovely San Miguel Valley. However, to the south the road begins to climb, gradually at first, following the sparkling San Miguel River in a southeasterly direction. Soon it becomes steeper, and as you leave the confines of the red rock canyon, you can see the San Miguel Mountains and the 14,017-foot pyramid of Wilson Peak to the south. Continuing on, you come to Telluride via a short spur road off the main highway.

Telluride used to be a quiet little town of great charm and character. But a massive ski area and numerous land developments have changed it quite drastically. The name *Telluride*, incidentally, is derived from the element tellurium, found here in conjunction with gold. The town was once one of the state's most active gold camps, and the bank here was robbed by Butch Cassidy and his gang in 1889.

South of the Telluride turnoff, Highway 145 continues to climb up to and past the old boom town of Ophir (named for the biblical location of King Solomon's mines), where it turns southwest. There are sensational views along this route of Mount Wilson and Wilson Peak in the San Miguel Mountains.

Beyond Ophir, you come to Lizard Head Pass (elevation 10,222 feet) at the beginning of the Dolores River drainage. From here, the road drops down and follows the river as it swells in volume from its numerous tributaries. A few miles down the pass is the turnoff for Dunton and the West Dolores River, described next. Staying on Highway 145, you'll go through the town of Rico, with its scarred and denuded hillsides. Gold and silver were mined here in the 1870s, and Rico (Spanish for "rich") once boasted six thousand inhabitants. The mining conducted in the area today is for lead, zinc, and copper.

South of Rico, the Dolores becomes a swift and sizable river, and you may see both kayakers and rafting parties challenging the fast waters.

Dunton

The drive to Dunton is short enough to be taken as an extension of the Telluride and Dolores River trip. But this isn't your typical side excursion, for Dunton is a special place. So special, in fact, that I include it here with great reluctance.

When you leave Telluride and head south on Colorado Highway 145, you begin the long climb to the top of Lizard Head Pass. As you start down the south side of the pass, keep a sharp eye out for an obscure road on the right and a sign reading "Dunton." This road climbs sharply from Highway 145 and winds through a glorious grove of aspen. It is a dirt road, rough in places, but passable for most cars. (I think I'd hesitate to attempt pulling a camping trailer or driving a low-slung car over it.)

After winding up over another small pass and down a forested hillside, the road parallels the West Dolores River. This lovely stream—it hardly appears to be a river at this point—meanders gently through open willow flats and spruce forests before joining the Dolores River west of Stoner. About eight miles from where you turned off Highway 145, you will arrive at the former gold-mining town of Dunton.

When we described Dunton in the first edition of *Backroads of Colorado*, this collection of old log buildings—a store, a saloon, some cabins, and a hotel—was operated as a resort. Well, perhaps "resort" was a euphemism. It was really pretty funky, but delightful. There's a wonderful hot springs here that used to be housed in a decrepit old building (why worry about a leaking roof when you're immersed in a pool of one-hundred-degree water?). And the cabins were . . . well, usable. There was a special character to the place, and the valley still has a feeling of isolation. Small wonder that Butch Cassidy and his gang made it a point to stop in Dunton after robbing the bank over in Telluride in 1889. You used to be able to sip a drink in the old saloon and rub elbows with the ghost of the infamous outlaw himself.

But no more. Sadly the place is now a private club that is closed to the public. You can, however, still enjoy the beauty of this valley of the West Dolores River. Much of this land is soft and gentle, reminding me of parts of New England. And the autumns here, like those in New England, are spectacular. A most magnificent place.

The road eventually joins Highway 145 at the Dolores River, well west of Rico and Stoner.

Hovenweep National Monument

One of my favorite places in all of Colorado is Hovenweep National Monument, though only half of it is in the state. The other half is in Utah. Furthermore, the monument is not one single area, but consists of six scattered clusters of ruins, two in Utah and four in Colorado.

The best way to get there is from Cortez, in the southwest corner of Colorado. Here, U.S. Highway 666 heads northwest and eventually leads into Utah. However, long before reaching the state line and about twenty miles from Cortez, you pass through the little town of Pleasant View. Follow the signs here to the monument. The road runs straight west and then generally southwest.

This is arid country. It's also flat, open country with distant views of the mountains to the east. In the spring, there is quite a contrast between the freshly plowed, brilliant red soil and the green of newly sprouted crops. Eventually you leave the last of the irrigated farmland and travel through juniper and piñon forests with fragrant sagebrush growing in profusion.

About twenty-three miles from Pleasant View,

The 14,246-foot-high Mount Wilson and the San Miguel Mountains viewed from Lizard Head Pass

and just inside Utah, you'll arrive at the small ranger station at the Square Tower Ruins, the largest and best preserved of the six units—and the most accessible. Before doing any exploring, you should go inside to learn the significance of this place. There's a campground nearby, but you'll have to bring your own equipment.

Hovenweep was the home of a pre-Columbian Native America people believed to be the ancestors of the modern-day Pueblos. They were related to, and perhaps even traded with, the residents of Mesa Verde some thirty miles to the southeast. Unlike the Mesa Verde people, however, the inhabitants of Hovenweep did not enjoy the security of massive cliff dwellings; the flatness of the land here is broken only by shallow canyons carved into the buff-colored sandstone. Instead, these people had to build smaller structures from flat rocks on the edges of canyons and gullies.

To me, the appeal of Hovenweep is the sense of history and tragedy it imparts. It is almost never crowded, and you can wander about by yourself, find your own private ruin, and sit quietly listening to the ghosts of a distant past. Naturally, you are expected to leave things as they are, and souvenir collecting is strictly prohibited.

The area was first inhabited around the time of the birth of Christ by nomads in search of small game and forage, who built small, temporary shelters of wooden poles and mud. Later, from about 900 A.D. to 1200 A.D., these people constructed more solid, permanent structures of rock, which offered some protection against hostile intruders. They also began to grow crops to alleviate their dependence on far-ranging and sparse game as their food staple.

The people survived quite well in this harsh land until about 1276 A.D. (a date established by tree-ring dating). That year marked the onset of a twenty-three-year drought that eventually—along with internal disagreements and invasions by outside groups—forced the inhabitants of Mesa Verde, Hovenweep, and other places to leave their ancestral lands and migrate south to wetter regions in the Rio Grande and Gila River valleys. The people never returned, and the ruins of their dwellings stand as a sad and silent monument to a natural disaster.

In visiting Hovenweep, allow plenty of time to roam about the clusters of ruins and the canyons. It seems a harsh, barren place at first, but there are touches of beauty to be found, especially in May and June, when the desert flowers are in bloom.

Incidentally, even though you won't find them on

Anasazi ruins dating from circa 600 A.D. in the Hovenweep National Monument

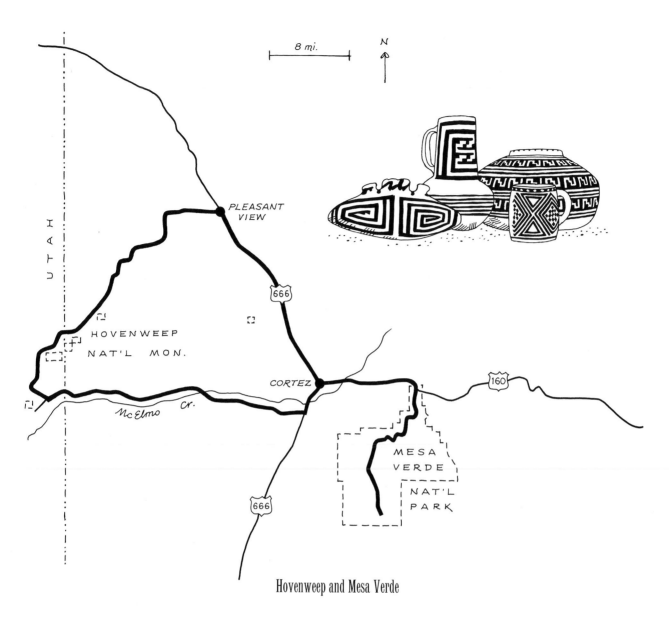

Hovenweep and Mesa Verde

your map, there are roads leading to all the ruins. But except for the one that took you to the ranger station, they are dirt roads that may be washed out in bad weather.

To return to Cortez and to the vicinity of Mesa Verde National Park for a highly recommended side trip, follow the McElmo Canyon road east to U.S. 666 and then head north a few miles to Cortez. About nine miles east of Cortez on U.S. Highway 160 is the entrance to the park (sixteen miles south of here is the Visitor Center). Mesa Verde is much larger, and more crowded than Hovenweep, and you are allowed to visit the cliff dwellings only on Park Service–guided tours. But even though a drive to the park hardly qualifies as an adventuresome backroad trip, you shouldn't pass it up, for the Mesa Verde ruins are even more impressive than those at Hovenweep.

To see the best-preserved Anasazi ruins, take a tour through the Ute Mountain Tribal Park. This little-known area, administered by the Utes, has five times the number of sites as Mesa Verde, is twice its size, and, best of all, has a fraction of the visitors. This new park, which wraps around two sides of Mesa Verde, was opened to visitors in 1982. While visitors may drive their own cars, a Ute guide must accompany all vehicles to the sites as a safety measure and as a means of assuring protection of the ruins. This is no drawback, since the guides are knowledgeable in the culture and the history of the Anasazi. However, reservations are necessary and can be arranged through the Cortez Visitor Information Center. The guided tours leave from the Ute Mountain Pottery Plant fifteen miles south of Cortez on U.S. Highway 666.

The Drought

When the first of the dry years came, the people thought, "Just one of these years. It'll break." But the drought didn't break. Each year the farmers would plant and hope for the spring rains. Sometimes a shower or two would allow the seeds to sprout, sending up tiny green shoots that would shrivel to brown threads when no more rain fell.

After a while the men stopped going to the fields each morning. There was nothing to do there anyway, and the sight of the brown, caked earth was heartbreaking. They hung around town, in small groups, talking mostly about the weather, and feeling idle and useless.

It was partly out of boredom, partly to seek the comfort of others in a similar situation, that one farmer traveled every week to the town from his house many miles away. He, like most of the men in the community, had been born and brought up on farming. In the past, his skill had been enough to give his family a good living. Now the weather and the land were betraying him. So he joined the other farmers in town as they talked and tried to think of something to do.

It was perhaps even worse for the farmer's wife. Each morning she'd go to the door of the two-story house and look out to see the same hot, dry landscape and the same blazing sun. She'd know that her husband would be even more depressed and the children even more fretful. And each day she faced the impossible task of stretching the diminishing food supply a little further. Still, she tried to be gay and cheerful and optimistic. Someone in the family had to be, and besides, the drought couldn't last forever.

As the months went by with no relief, her optimism seemed pointless and, indeed, ludicrous. Her bright chatter didn't cheer up her husband, and the baby cried no matter how much she cuddled him. So even she gave up and retreated into a worried silence.

It was the young people of the area who were the first to move. It was easier for them to just pick up and go. "We just can't make it here anymore. There's no future," they said. The older ones sadly agreed. A few of the braver families also went. When the town's water supply began to dry up, it

The cliff palace at Mesa Verde (Photo courtesy of Library, The State Historical Society of Colorado)

was no longer a question of "Are you going to move?" but "When are you going to move and where?"

The farmer came home from one of his weekly visits to the town one day with the news that several families had decided to stick together and move as a group. That way, maybe they'd have a better chance at a fresh start in a new place. The farmer and his wife talked it over and decided to go with them. It was a hard decision. Both had spent their entire lives in this same community. As had their parents and grandparents.

On moving day, after all their belongings were packed up, the farmer's wife carefully swept out the empty and echoing rooms. Someday, she hoped, they'd be able to return.

A few stubborn ones remained in the town. "The rains will come," they insisted. "They always have. A drought's never lasted this long before." Soon, even these optimists saw the futility of staying. The village became a ghost town.

The drought lasted for twenty-four years. The people never returned.

In 1874, photographer William Henry Jackson was traveling in the neighborhood and came across the farmer's abandoned house. The family had been gone for seven hundred years. It was the first documented discovery of the fabulous cliff dwellings of the Anasazi people who inhabited the region of Mesa Verde and the Ute Mountain Tribal Park.

Clouds sailing over the plains near Pawnee Buttes

Part III
The Great Plains

▲▲▲▲▲

We all seem to have preferences for—or perhaps prejudices against—certain landforms. There are desert rats, who love nothing better than the sunseared land of sand, cactus, and slickrock. Mountain folks never quite seem comfortable away from their rocky ramparts, deep winter snows, and color-splashed tundra. For others, the pounding, moody seacoasts are home. And then there are the flatlanders, who like their land uncluttered, free, and open, where the vast expanse of sky can be scrutinized for clues of the day-after-tomorrow's weather.

Lone windmill on the Great Plains

For those who love mountains or for whom deserts have quickly grasped charm, the prairies are definitely an acquired taste. But it's not hard to learn to love this land, or at least to appreciate it. Perhaps Willa Cather in *Death Comes for the Archbishop* best describes the character of the flatlands:

> Elsewhere the sky is the roof of the world; but here the earth was the floor of the sky. The landscape one longed for when one was far away, the thing all about one, the work one actually lived in, was the sky, the sky!

Mention Colorado, and most people think of mountains. Yet more than a third of the state lies in the domain of the Great Plains, that vast sweep of prairie extending eastward from the Rockies to the Mississippi. In many ways this flatland of eastern Colorado has more of an Old West flavor than the High Country. This is the land of the Plains Indians—the Pawnee, the Cheyenne, the Comanche, the Arapaho. It's still possible here to sense the expansiveness that awed the mountain men, the members of the Pike and Long expeditions, the gold seekers, and the immigrant settlers. This is Kit Carson country, former home of the bison, cattle barons, and sodbusters, rich in history, tinged with irony, marked with tragedy. Earth, sky, grass, cactus, yucca all come together here. Short grass prairie, tall grass prairie. A land where much of the original prairie has been tamed, changed to farming and ranching country with irrigation, and where oil wells sprout amid the crops and browsing cattle.

For a land that seems so stark and barren—it was once called the "great American desert"—it can be rich

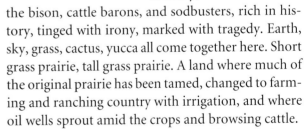

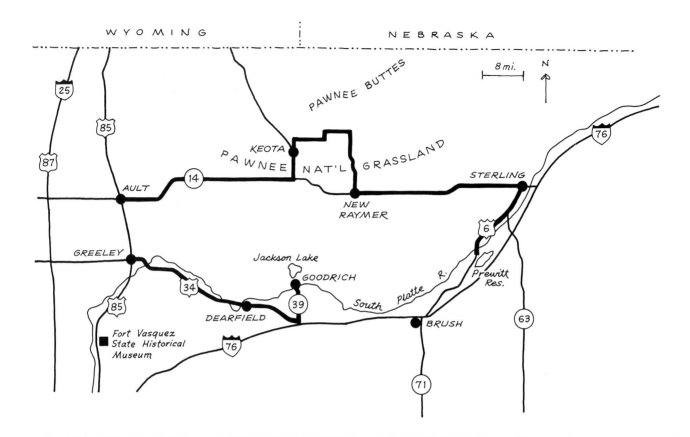

Pawnee National Grassland and the South Platte River

and fecund. Gentle springs with yellow cactus blossoms, creamy yucca flowers, new green grass, and the smell of sweet damp earth. Amber autumns, the mellow season of waving grass and grain, and the sounds of geese and duck heading south once more. There are more than 150 species of birds, ranging from prairie falcon and golden eagle to sandhill crane, meadowlark, and blackcapped chickadee. The bison are gone, at least the immense numbers of them that once roamed here, but the pronghorn antelope, once near extinction, are thriving. From rattlesnake to prairie dog, many of the original inhabitants are still here.

Because it is a more subtle land, traveling the backroads of the Great Plains requires time—time, that is, to stop and roam a bit to see, smell, and hear the prairie. In some places, a sense of historical perspective can be realized only by leaving car and road far behind and out of sight. But sometimes it's necessary to wander only a short distance to absorb the essence of the prairie, to learn what it's all about.

Like the Western Slopes, this section of the state usually enjoys early springs and late autumns. But for a terrain so simple, the weather in the Great Plains can have its violent aspects. Although summer storms are severe enough in the High Country, they sometimes have a special ferocity in the flatlands. Hot, searing summers, with afternoon thunderstorms moving across the open lands in ponderous, billowing black clouds, blasting rains into the parched soil with ear-shattering, heart-pounding thunder and lightning. Cold winters, with biting winds and drifting snows. And although they may be rare in the mountains, tornadoes are not at all uncommon in eastern Colorado.

In traveling the backroads of the plains, it's best to keep an eye on the weather. Fortunately, the uncluttered view while you're driving makes this easy, giving you ample warning of approaching storms sometimes hours before they hit. It's a good idea also to listen to a local station on the car radio if the impending storm looks particularly ominous, for tornado warnings may be given under these conditions. Regardless of the estimated severity of the forecast, you may want to think about heading back to a main highway. Even the briefest of thunderstorms can

Pawnee Buttes

transform a dusty backroad into an impassable quagmire. I spent one long afternoon out near the Pawnee Buttes trying to drive a rain-soaked road that had turned to axle-deep mud.

Unlike the High Country, much of the land in this part of the state is privately owned, the exception being the Pawnee and Comanche National Grasslands (under the jurisdiction of the U.S. Forest Service, in case you want more information). Fences and roads of farms and ranches should be respected. It is usually possible to obtain permission from farmers and ranchers to roam about on some of their land, and while you're conversing with them, you'll often hear fascinating stories of local history. These are people proud of their land, with a strong appreciation for its subtle beauty.

Pawnee National Grassland

This trip begins at Ault, on Colorado Highway 14 about ten miles north of Greeley. The road heads east through rolling, gentle farm country, then enters Pawnee National Grassland, a 772,000-acre area of low, grass-covered hills and sandstone buttes. At first, there seems to be little difference between the farmland around Ault and the grassland, but soon it's obvious that this is uncultivated and unirrigated country, for it's much drier than the lush wheat fields to the west.

In the 1930s, the U.S. government bought the farms and ranches from the homesteaders who wanted to leave the dust bowl, and then began reseeding the purchased land so it would once again have a protective covering of grass. The people who wanted to stay on here were encouraged to convert to cattle ranching. Today, as a result of the government program, most of Pawnee National Grassland is covered by blue grama and buffalo grass, the short prairie grasses native to the region. Over half of the area is still privately owned, but the land is now being used primarily for grazing sheep and cattle.

The grassland is ornithologist Roger Tory Peterson's favorite place in all of Colorado, and it didn't take me long to discover why. The blue grama and buffalo grass support a huge bird population. I

saw mountain plovers, prairie falcons, and Swainson's hawks, to name a few, and you can expect to see countless other species. (According to the U.S. Department of Agriculture, at last 225 different species of birds have been sighted here since 1962.)

About midway between Ault and Sterling, I turned north on a gravel road and followed signs to Keota. This once-thriving community is a virtual ghost town. The dry winds blow tumbleweeds outside of town. It's ironic that the name *Keota* is derived from an Indian word meaning "gone to visit."

From here I followed numerous dirt roads north and east to different parts of the Pawnee Buttes, the sandstone and chalk cliffs that rise above the rest of the grassland. The buttes were among the first places in Colorado to be studied by paleontologists, and many fossils of plains animals have been found in the sandstone strata.

This is country to explore on foot. I wandered up sandy draws, smelling the sweet pungent aroma of sagebrush and looking for yellow cactus blossoms. The landscape was dotted with swordlike yucca plants, and in one of those dry creek beds, I came upon a beautiful bull snake.

In the walls of the buttes are many caves and alcoves. I enjoyed sitting here alone, imagining Cheyenne or Arapahoe lookouts watching for bison or enemy tribes for this same spot. And far on the distant horizon, I could see the shimmering snow of Longs Peak.

Above: *Lonely tree near Pawnee National Grassland*
Left: *Thunderclouds above the prairie near Pawnee National Grassland*

The Mountain Men

In a great many ways, the fur trappers and traders collectively known as the mountain men were a tougher, lustier breed than the miners or prospectors who followed them several decades later. Some of their names have become legend: Jim Bridger, Jedediah Smith, Kit Carson, Jim Beckwourth.

The two decades from 1820 to 1840 represented the golden era of the mountain men. It was a whim of fashion in Europe and the Eastern United States—beaver hats—that created a demand for their skills, although other furs were also popular. Roaming far and wide throughout the Rocky Mountain area and beyond, they trapped beavers and sold the pelts at the annual summer rendezvous, where they combined business with all around hell raising.

Some were loners, "free trappers." Others worked for such companies as John Jacob Astor's American Fur Company (known simply as "The Company"), the Rocky Mountain Fur Company (owned for a while by Jedediah Smith, William L. Sublette, and David E. Jackson, for whom Jackson Hole, in Wyoming, is named), the Hudson's Bay Company, or General William H. Ashley's firm. Ashley employed about three hundred men in the West.

It was with Ashley that Jedediah Smith, probably the greatest mountain man of them all, got his start. Unlike most of the fur trappers, Smith was a well-educated and religious man, who toted a Bible and a volume of Shakespeare's plays in his pack. Other Ashley employees were Beckwourth and the legendary Mike Fink. During a rendezvous, Fink killed his buddy in a shooting match. He claimed it was an accident—they were both drunk—but he must not have been convincing, for to this day many people regard his name as the origin for the word meaning "treacherous" or "contemptible." Later Fink himself met a violent death while on one of Ashley's fur-trapping expeditions. Beckwourth, the son of a Virginia planter and a black slave, gave up trapping to live with the Crow, eventually becoming a war chief. He had convinced them he was one of them, that he'd been kidnapped as a child.

It was a dangerous way of life. The trappers lived off the land and at times the land was

Mountain man Kit Carson from an engraving in John Frémont's Memoirs of My Life *(Photo courtesy of Library, The State Historical Society of Colorado)*

unforgiving of mistakes in judgment. More than a few of them died of starvation, froze to death, or drowned in a raging river. Grizzly bears, plentiful inhabitants of the Rockies then, killed or maimed others. At this time, the Rocky Mountain West was still largely terra incognita, the only knowledge of the terrain provided by the expeditions led by Meriwether Lewis and William Clark from 1804–1806, and by Zebulon Pike and Stephen H. Long in 1806 and 1820 respectively.

The mountain men, in their extensive wanderings, discovered many of the natural wonders of the West long before they were "discovered" decades later by government expeditions. When John Colter, who left the Lewis and Clark Expedition to go into fur trapping, described the geysers and hot springs in what is now Yellowstone National Park—he is credited with being the first white man to see them— no one believed him. "Colter's Hell," his "hallucinations" were called. Nor did Jim Bridger fare any better a little later. His descriptions of the same area were dubbed "Bridger's lies."

Not only was the wilderness itself an adversary, but certain Native American tribes, the Blackfeet in particular, were hostile and brutal in their dealings with the trappers. Many mountain men lost their lives and scalps at the hands of the Indians.

Was it worth the danger? Did they earn enough

money to compensate for such perils and privations? Whereas potential wealth may have been their initial incentive, history has shown that few of the trappers made much money from their dangerous ventures. The real fortunes were made by the owners of the fur companies, such as John Jacob Astor, in their towers of Eastern commerce. For the mountain men, however, there were other rewards. Warren Angus Ferris was employed by Astor's American Fur Company in 1830. He kept meticulous journals of his adventures and in one made this observation:

> The very danger has its attractions, and the courage and cunning, and skill, and watchfulness made necessary by the difficulties [the mountain men] have to overcome, the privations they are forced to contend with, and the perils against which they must guard, become at once their pride and boast. A strange, wild, terrible, romantic, hard and exciting life they lead, with alternate plenty and starvation, activity and repose, safety and alarm, and all the other adjuncts that belong to so vagrant a condition in a harsh, barren, untamed and fearful region of desert, plain and mountain. Yet so attached to it do they become that few ever leave it.

Some mountain men were inveterate wanderers. Crossing country that had never been explored by white men before, Jedediah Smith twice trekked to California and back, the second journey so perilous that it cost the lives of most of his companions. After a final, highly profitable fur-trapping expedition, he tried to quit but couldn't. While leading a wagon train to Santa Fe in 1831—a job he had volunteered for—the great trailblazer was ambushed by a band of Comanches and killed, but not before the redoubtable Smith had dispatched several of his attackers.

By the early 1840s, heavy trapping had almost exterminated the beaver. Meanwhile, more permanent fur-trading establishments had been built in Colorado. Fort Vasquez, constructed in 1837 by Louis Vasquez and Andrew Sublette near present-day Denver, was one of these. More important was Bent's Old Fort, completed in 1833, on the north bank of the Arkansas River (see "Bent's Old Fort").

The declining years of the fur trade overlapped the westward migration of settlers and gold seekers. Bent's Fort was fortuitously located on the Santa Fe Trail and became an important stopping point for travelers and for traders handling goods of every description. Former mountain men such as Kit Carson became scouts: Carson served three of John Charles Frémont's expeditions across Colorado in the 1840s. During the Civil War he served in the Union Army, rising to the brevet rank of brigadier general.

The era of the mountain men was one of the most colorful in Rocky Mountain history. In his book, *Across the Wide Missouri*, Bernard DeVoto describes the excitement and danger of their way of life:

> The mountain men were a tough race, as many selective breeds of Americans have had to be; their courage, skill, and mastery of the conditions of their chosen life were absolute or they would not have been here. Nor would they have been here if they had not responded to the loveliness of the country and found . . . something precious beyond safety, gain, comfort, and family life.

Adobe farmhouse in Boggsville, home of Kit Carson for many years

Few of the roads north of Keota are marked, but that makes taking them much more of an adventure. There's little danger of getting lost, for you can always backtrack. On one of these obscure lanes, I came over a rise to surprise a small herd of pronghorn antelope. They raced along in front of the car, and I clocked them at thirty-five miles per hour before they veered off toward the foothills.

My blunderings eventually took me to New Raymer and Highway 14 again, then on to Sterling.

Along the South Platte River

When I left Sterling, turning right on U.S. Highway 6, I expected the jaunt southeast along the South Platte River to be quick and uneventful. Although the trip looks short on the map (it's only about twenty miles), you can spend a lot of time poking around the bottomlands, as I did. The road is quieter than you would expect, for U.S. 6, once the main highway from Denver to Sterling to Nebraska and points east, has been supplanted in Colorado by Interstate 76—one of those cases where a main highway has now become a backroad.

The name Platte was bestowed on the river by some early French trappers, who called it Riviére la Platte, meaning "shallow river" or "thin river." And shallow it is. In fact, the stream is broken into numerous channels and sloughs, each of them shallow enough to wade.

There is a strong sense of history along this stretch of the river. Perhaps a few of the magnificent old cottonwoods in the area were saplings when Kit Carson, Bill Williams, and other fur trappers followed the South Platte toward old Fort Vasquez between present-day Denver and Greeley in the 1830s. Seven miles south of Sterling, just east of U.S. 6 on Colorado Highway 63, a state historical marker directs you to a monument on the site of Summit Springs battleground. At the springs, southeast of here, the U.S. cavalry and 150 Pawnee scouts, guided by Buffalo Bill Cody, surprised and overwhelmed the Cheyenne in the last (July 1869) Plains Indian battle fought in the state. Chief Tall Bull and his "Dog Soldiers" had been

Above: *South Platte River cutting through the Great Plains*
Opposite: *Yucca blossoms near the site of the Sand Creek Massacre*

Big Sandy Creek

When I turned off Colorado Highway 71 at Limon and drove southeast on U.S. 287, I knew where I was heading. My destination was the site of the infamous Sand Creek Massacre, on Big Sandy Creek. What I didn't expect when I got there was the powerful impact this place would have on me.

At the town of Kit Carson, the road turns right and south to Eads. Heading east from here, I looked for signs pointing the way to the massacre site. A couple of miles east of Chivington, I spotted a stone historical marker indicating that the tragedy had taken place about twelve miles north of this spot, so I wheeled off the highway and followed the gravel road in that direction. Fortunately, a few small signs had been erected near the site of the battle, for otherwise I might have spent several hours bouncing over the myriad dusty roads in the area.

I think it is fortunate that you can't drive directly to Big Sandy Creek. Instead, you must park on a sand hill, where there's another small marker, and walk a quarter of a mile or so down into the little valley. The vulnerability of the camp's location among those old cottonwoods is apparent as you amble down from the rise of land where the U.S. Army troops launched their attack.

What did happen here? On the morning of November 29, 1864, Colonel John Chivington and several hundred of his men mounted a surprise attack on the combined Arapahoe and Cheyenne encampment along Big Sandy Creek. Expecting hundreds of armed warriors, Chivington discovered mainly old men, women, and children among the 600 Indians camped here. Nonetheless, the slaughter took place. When it was over, 105 women and children and 28 men in the camp lay dead, while 9 of Chivington's soldiers died. The brutality was compounded when many of the Indian dead were scalped and some mutilated.

Today, Big Sandy Creek is an intermittent little stream, as it undoubtedly was then, flowing quietly through sand country. The plains are quite dry here, almost desert. Along the creek bottom are immense cottonwoods. It is a lovely spot, but I had a decided feeling of tragedy, a sense of malevolent history as I wandered around. I spent a long time sitting among the trees, roaming up and down the stream, listening to the breeze stir the cottonwood leaves. The June sun was hot and it was a pleasant day, but I decided to leave rather than camp. There were just too many troubled

Big Sandy Creek, site of the infamous Sand Creek Massacre of 1864

raiding Kansas and Colorado settlements.

Where U.S. 6 crosses over to the south bank of the river, another tablet marks the site of Old Fort Wicked. This Overland Stage station and stockade was the only one in the South Platte area to survive the Indian attacks during a rampage along the one-hundred-mile stretch. The station master, H. Godfrey, put up such a good fight that the Indians nicknamed him "Old Wicked."

On the south side of the river, U.S. 6 leads to Prewitt Reservoir. Along the western shore of the reservoir, set amid more lovely old cottonwoods, there's an excellent campground. For the evening's entertainment, I watched a flock of white pelicans skimming the water and swooping in precision aerial acrobatics. The bird life here is astounding. Besides the pelicans, I spotted meadowlarks, ospreys, great blue herons, and several species of ducks.

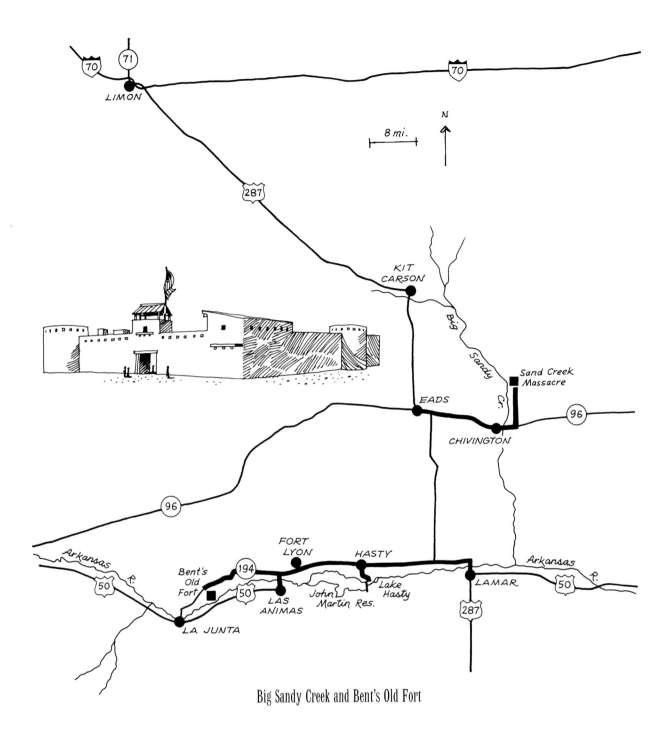

Big Sandy Creek and Bent's Old Fort

spirits here. A sad piece of history for Colorado and the nation.

Bent's Old Fort

A good place to begin this tour to Bent's Old Fort is at Lamar, a small town at the juncture of U.S. Highway 50 and U.S. 287. On Main Street is the Madonna of the Trail monument, a statue memorializing the pioneer mothers whose sacrifices made possible the settling of the West.

Leaving Lamar, first head north for a short distance, and then west on U.S. 50, which parallels the Arkansas River. At Hasty, turn south onto an unmarked road that crosses the river and leads to the John Martin Reservoir. This access road runs between the 645,500-acre reservoir, the largest in Colorado, and manmade Lake Hasty. There's a first-rate campground near the recreational lake, where you can fish or just relax and enjoy the view.

Retrace your way back to U.S. 50—it's a short drive—and continue west past Fort Lyon, a Veterans

Above: *Cottonwood trees growing along a stream course*
running through the prairie near Greeley
Left: *Foxtail barley bending to the wind along the*
Arkansas River near Bent's Old Fort

Administration Hospital; on the grounds is the cabin where Kit Carson lived and died and which now serves as a chapel. A few miles farther west, at the intersection of Colorado Highway 194 and U.S. 50, turn south to Las Animas, worth a visit to browse through the Kit Carson Museum with its many exhibits, including mementos of the famed scout; the pioneer jail and rural schoolhouse are part of the museum. William Bent is buried in the town cemetery. Double back the mile or so north to Highway 194, and about ten miles west of the turnoff, you'll come to Bent's Old Fort.

Charles and William Bent and their partner, Ceran St. Vrain, made a smart decision when they chose the northern banks of the Arkansas River, near present-day La Junta, as the site for their fort and trading post. The Mountain Branch of the Santa Fe Trail ran along the river through western Kansas and eastern Colorado, then veered southwest at the spot where the fort was built to enter New Mexico over Raton Pass. In the early 1820s, U.S. merchants had become interested in trading with Mexico, which then controlled New Mexico. The land along the Arkansas River was the domain of the Plains Indians, who roamed far and wide in pursuit of buffalo, and of the mountain men, those hardy fur trappers who followed the Arkansas and South Platte Rivers to the Rockies. Thus the fort was accessible to traders, Indians, and fur trappers alike.

Bent's Fort was completed in 1833, though the huge structure was in use for some time before this. For sixteen years, it was the largest and most important trading center in the Southwest. It was an ideal place of exchange for goods being transported east and west: cloth, ammunition, beads, and supplies shipped from the Mississippi Valley; buffalo robes, beaver pelts, silver, horses, and blankets shipped east. It was also a natural stopover for those following the Santa Fe Trail and a popular social center for Indians, plainsmen, mountain men, and traders. Before the fort was abandoned and partially demolished in 1849, many of the heroes of the Old West—Jim Bridger, Jim "Medicine Calf" Beckwourth, R. L. "Uncle Dick" Wootton, Kit Carson, and John C. Frémont, among others—either worked or passed through here.

Under the auspices of the National Park Service, the old adobe fort has been reconstructed on its original site, and it is a fascinating place to visit, even if

Above: *The blacksmith shop at Bent's Old Fort*
Opposite: *Doorway at Bent's Old Fort*

you're not a history buff. As you approach this imposing structure, you'll understand why more than one frontier traveler likened it to a medieval castle. Its fourteen-foot-high walls, twin round towers, and square watchtower give it the appearance of impregnability, an impression that is heightened when you pass through its tunnel-like entrance.

Allow plenty of time to explore the inside of the fort, for there is a great deal to see. The entire area enclosed by the outer walls is larger than a football field. As soon as you pass through the entrance way, you'll notice a square of rooms, each facing an inner courtyard. In the well-marked information center on the ground floor of the quadrangle, you can obtain a map of the structure and a brochure explaining its extraordinary history. Most of the fort's thirty-three rooms have been furnished with antiques or reproductions of antique furniture from the 1830s. And if you plan your trip for the summer months, you'll be able to see "living history" demonstrations of frontier cooking, carpentry, and blacksmithing.

When you've finished touring the huge complex, you can mosey down to the Arkansas and listen to the music of flowing water. Chances are you'll find yourself lost in thought, ruminating as I did, on the colorful and tragic lives of Charles Bent, who conceived the idea of the fort, and his brother William, who managed and destroyed it.

The Bents and Their Fort

Gone. They're all dead and gone, William Bent thought as he walked through the empty rooms of the fort. Three brothers. A wife. Half the southern Cheyenne—his friends.

William stooped to pick up a broken teacup from a pile of rubble. He remembered when it had arrived from St. Louis: An attempt to bring civilization to the wild frontier. He laughed, remembering how the mountain men and Cheyenne had teased him about becoming soft.

Maybe he had. He sure wasn't as tough as he had been in the 1820s when he started working with his brother, Charles. You had to be tough to survive in those early days of the fur-trading business, what with the Indian attacks, blizzards, and starvation. Of course, that was many years ago, when he was only a kid. Now, in 1849, he was forty years old.

There had been a lot of changes out here in the West during that time. He'd even been responsible for a few changes himself. This fort, for instance.

When he, Charles, and Ceran St. Vrain had formed their company, there was no trading post or fort on the Santa Fe Trail. The freighters loaded their wagons in Missouri and made a beeline for Santa Fe or Taos, hoping they would make it. They were at the mercy of the weather and Indians alike.

The fort had been Charles's idea. "Think what we could do with a post along the route," he'd said. "We could use it for protection and storage, and the Indians could come to us to trade their buffalo robes. And that's where the money's going to be in the future—buffalo robes, not beaver skins."

Yes, Charles had been the planner. But he, William, was the builder. Adobe was the logical building material, he'd decided, because it was fireproof, and besides there wasn't enough timber available on the treeless plains for the sprawling fortress he had in mind. With one hundred or so Mexican laborers working for him, it had taken a couple of years before the structure was completed.

William ran his hand over the smooth adobe wall. He remembered the day he'd ridden a couple of miles out onto the prairie, then turned around to look at the almost completed building. Why, it looks like one of those huge old castles, right out of England or France or maybe Spain, he thought.

And he recalled how enormously pleased he had been.

So had Charles. "It's to be called William's Fort," he declared, but the name hadn't stuck. The mountain men called it Bent's Fort, so Bent's Fort it was. Which was only right, William reflected. Sure, he was the resident manager, but his brothers Robert and George had also worked hard to make the trading company a success.

And it had been a success. With him managing the fort, and Charles and St. Vrain taking care of the business end at Taos and Santa Fe, their firm had become the largest trading company in the area served by the Santa Fe Trail.

You know, I wasn't a bad manager, William decided. It hadn't been easy, handling mountain men, Indians, soldiers, emigrants, and other assorted travelers who stopped at the fort.

He felt especially proud that the Indians had trusted him. I was fair with them, he thought, that's why. I was fair with them, I understood them, and I liked them. No, I loved them. Especially the Cheyenne.

Especially Owl Woman. She had been so beautiful when he married her. She'd given him three children, then died when the fourth was born.

Stop it! William said to himself. Stop this confounded remembering! That part of my life is over, and the dead won't come back. Not Owl Woman. Not Robert, killed by a Comanche. Not George, dead of disease. Not all my Cheyenne friends, killed by the cholera epidemic brought by the emigrants. Not even Charles.

Charles. More father than older brother. Killed in Taos by a screaming mob of Mexicans and Indians, while his wife and children watched.

The good old U.S. Army was to blame, William thought bitterly. If the government hadn't started the war with Mexico and sent the army out here to capture New Mexico and California, Charles would be alive.

William was angry now. First, the army had come marching right up to the fort and taken it over as if they owned it. Then they had expected him to provide food for them, to entertain the officers, to supply forage for the horses. Never mind that they were ruining the trading business, that their presence was driving the Indians away.

Then, after the army had captured New Mexico, they made Charles governor of the new

American territory, but left him defenseless in Santa Fe while they marched off to California. How did they expect him to keep the natives from revolting when he had no troops?

Everything had changed. St. Vrain left the company. Got out just in time. They never saw eye-to-eye—it was Charles who had kept the firm together. And business kept getting worse. Still, for a while there'd been enough trading to keep the place going.

"Well, Charles is dead, and Bent, St. Vrain, and Company is dead," William said aloud. "I've got a new wife and a baby on the way. I'm starting a new life. But I can't do it here with all you ghosts around, do you understand?" His voice echoed through the empty building. "I can't live here anymore. The army wants to buy the fort but won't pay me what it's worth. I can't let it fall into the hands of the Indians to use in a suicidal war against the whites. There's nothing else to do."

Swiftly he rolled the powder kegs into the main rooms. Then he set fire to the wooden roof and all the refuse that had been left behind. He had ridden halfway to the camp, where his family and a few employees were waiting, when the powder kegs exploded.

Bent's Fort was gone.

Bent moved his family thirty-eight miles downstream and built a new stone fort on the banks of the Arkansas River, in an area known as Big Timbers. But the second trading post was never as successful as the first had been in the 1830s, and eventually he leased it to the government.

William Bent lived for twenty years after he blew up the old fort. In that time, he would see war and disease almost exterminate the Native Americans he loved. He would see the surge of new white settlers to this land that was once thought uninhabitable for whites. He would agonize over the fate of his four children who were trapped along Big Sandy Creek when Colonel John Chivington attacked the Indian village there. And, when they survived the massacre, he would disown one of them for murdering whites with a savagery that disgusted whites and Indians alike.

Again and again during these years, William tried to bring peace between Native Americans and whites. He told the group of congressmen who were investigating the Sand Creek Massacre: "If the matter were left to me, I guarantee with my life that in three months I could have all the Indians along the Arkansas at peace without the expense of war."

Unfortunately, the U.S. government didn't listen to William Bent.

Bent's Old Fort stands again, reconstructed by the National Park Service. A national historic site, it serves as a monument not only to Charles and William Bent, but also to the times of which they were such an important part.

Drawing of Bent's Old Fort circa 1845 (Sketch courtesy National Park Service)

Suggestions For Further Reading

Since we first published *Backroads of Colorado*, there have been over two thousand books written about Colorado—and these are just the ones that are still in print. Since we can't list them all, here are a few, both old and new, that we think you might like.

Guidebooks

Brown, Robert L. *Colorado Ghost Towns, Past and Present.* Caldwell, Idaho: Caxton Printers, 1972.

Cahill, Rick. *Colorado Hot Springs Guide.* 2nd ed. rev. Boulder, Colorado: Pruett Publishing Company, 1994.

Conly, Marc and Nancy M. Conly. *Waterfalls of Colorado.* Boulder, Colorado: Pruett Publishing Company, 1993.

Green, Stewart. *Colorado Parklands.* Helena, Montana: Falcon Press, 1988.

Helmuth, Ed. *Passes of Colorado: An Encyclopedia of Watershed Divides.* Boulder, Colorado: Pruett Publishing Company, 1994.

Kleinsorge, Martin G. *Exploring Colorado State Parks.* Niwot, Colorado: University Press of Colorado, 1992.

Ormes, Robert M. *Guide to the Colorado Mountains.* 9th ed. rev. Denver: Colorado Mountain Club, 1992.

Parris, Lloyd. *Caves of Colorado.* Boulder, Colorado: Pruett Publishing Company, 1975.

Rennicke, Jeff. *Colorado Mountain Ranges.* Helena, Montana: Falcon Press, 1986.

_____. *Rivers of Colorado.* Helena, Montana: Falcon Press, 1985.

Spurr, Dick and Wendy Spurr. *Historic Forts of Colorado.* Grand Junction, Colorado: Centennial Publications, 1994.

The WPA Guide to 1930s Colorado. Compiled by Workers of the Writers' Program of the Work Projects Administration in the State of Colorado. Lawrence, Kansas: University Press of Kansas, 1987.

General

Bright, William. *Colorado Place Names.* Boulder, Colorado: Johnson Books, 1993.

Lavender, David. *David Lavender's Colorado.* New York: Doubleday, 1976.

Wood, Myron and Nancy C. Wood. *Colorado: Big Mountain Country.* Rev. ed. New York: Doubleday, 1972.

Worcester, Thomas K. and Robert B. Pamplin, Jr. *A Portrait of Colorado.* Beaverton, Oregon: Touchstone Press, 1976.

Natural History

Andrews, Robert and Robert Righter. *Colorado Birds.* Denver: Denver Museum of Natural History. 1992.

Bailey, Alfred M. and Robert J. Niedrach. *Birds of Colorado.* 2 vols. Denver: Denver Museum of Natural History, 1965.

Gray, Mary T. *Colorado Wildlife Viewing Guide.* Helena, Montana: Falcon Press, 1992.

Lechleitner, R. R. *Wild Mammals of Colorado: Their Appearance, Habits, Distribution, and Abundance.* Boulder, Colorado: Pruett Publishing Company, 1969.

Pearl, Richard M. *Colorado Rocks, Minerals, Fossils.* Denver: Sage Books, 1964.

Pesman, M. Walter. *Meet the Natives: The Amateur's Fieldguide to Rocky Mountain Wildflowers, Trees and Shrubs.* 9th ed. Boulder, Colorado: Roberts Rinehart Publishers, 1992.

Seacrest, Betty R. and Delbert A. McNew. *Rocky Mountain Birds: Easy Identification.* Boulder, Colorado: Avery Press, Inc., 1990.

Weber, William A. *Colorado Flora: Eastern Slope.* Boulder, Colorado: Colorado Associated University Press, 1990.

_____. *Colorado Flora: Western Slope.* Boulder, Colorado: Colorado Associated University Press, 1987.

History

Abbott, Carl, et. al. *Colorado: A History of the Centennial State.* 3rd ed. Niwot, Colorado: University of Colorado Press, 1994.

Bird, Isabella L. *A Lady's Life in the Rocky Mountains.*

The Western Frontier Library. Norman, Oklahoma: University of Oklahoma Press, 1960.

Blair, Edward. *Palace of Ice: A History of the Leadville Ice Palace of 1896.* Leadville, Colorado: Timberline Books, 1972.

Brown, Robert L. *Ghost Towns of the Colorado Rockies.* Caldwell, Idaho: Caxton Printers, 1968.

Brush, Helen N. and Catherine P. Dittman. *Indian Hills: The Place, the Times, the People.* 2nd ed. Englewood, Colorado: Graphic Impressions, Inc., 1993

Cassells, E. Steve. *The Archaeology of Colorado.* Boulder, Colorado: Johnson Books, 1983.

Ellis, Richard N. and Duane A. Smith. *Colorado: A History in Photographs.* Niwot, Colorado: University Press of Colorado, 1991.

Jackson, William H. and H. R. Driggs. *The Pioneer Photographer: Rocky Mountain Adventures with a Camera.* Yonkers-on-Hudson, New York: World Book Company, 1929.

Lanham, Urless N. *The Bone Hunters.* New York: Columbia University Press, 1973.

Lavender, David. *Bent's Fort.* New York: Doubleday, 1954.

Leonard, Stephen J. and Thomas J. Noel. *Denver: Mining Camp to Metropolis.* Niwot, Colorado: University Press of Colorado, 1990.

McGovern, George S. and Leonard F. Guttridge. *The Great Coalfield War.* Boston: Houghton Mifflin, 1972.

McTighe, James. *Roadside History of Colorado.* Boulder, Colorado: Johnson Books, 1989.

Mehls, Steven F. *The New Empire of the Rockies: A History of Northeast Colorado.* Denver: Bureau of Land Management, 1984.

Rippeteau, Bruce Estes. *A Colorado Book of the Dead: The Prehistoric Era.* Denver: Colorado Historical Society, 1979.

Shoemaker, Len. *Roaring Fork Valley.* 3rd ed. rev. Denver: Sundance, 1973.

Smith, P. David. *Ouray: Chief of the Utes.* Ouray, Colorado: Wayfinder Press, 1987.

Sprague, Marshall. *Colorado: A Bicentennial History.* New York: W. W. Norton, 1976.

_____. *Massacre: The Tragedy at White River.* Boston: Little, Brown, 1957.

_____. *Money Mountain: The Story of Cripple Creek Gold.* Boston: Little, Brown, 1953.

Sternberg, Gene and Barbara Sternberg. *Evergreen: Our Mountain Community.* Evergreen, Colorado: Sternberg and Sternberg. 2nd ed., 1993.

Ubbelohde, Carl, et. al. *A Colorado History.* 6th ed. Boulder, Colorado: Pruett Publishing Company, 1988.

William Henry Jackson's Colorado. Compiled by William C. Jones and Elizabeth B. Jones. Rev. ed. Golden, Colorado: Colorado Railroad Museum, 1992.

Wolle, Muriel Sibell. *Stampede to Timberline: The Ghost Towns and Mining Camps of Colorado.* 2nd ed. rev. Chicago: Swallow Press, 1974.

_____. *Timberline Tailings: Tales of Colorado's Ghost Towns and Mining Camps.* Chicago: The Swallow Press, Inc., 1977.

Index

About the Authors

Photo copyright © by Ed Borg

Boyd and Barbara Norton have lived in Colorado for nearly three decades. Both have traveled extensively in documenting the world's wild places and environmental issues, a specialty Boyd has pursued as a writer and photographer for more than twenty years. No stranger to hazardous assignments, he has photographed poisonous snakes, charging buffalo, cantankerous grizzly bears, whitewater rapids, mountain gorillas, and Moscow taxi drivers.

Boyd's articles and photo essays have appeared in many leading magazines, including *Time, National Geographic, Smithsonian, Audubon, Condé Nast's Traveler, Vogue,* and *Outdoor Photographer.* He is the author-photographer of many books, including *The Art of Outdoor Photography* (Voyageur Press) and *Baikal: Sacred Sea of Siberia.*

Barbara is the Manager of Product Information for Chronopol, Inc., a start-up company for the manufacture of biodegradable plastics. She has a master's degree in library science from the University of Denver.

Overleaf: *Pikes Peak viewed from Woodland Park*